09

10

13

11

12

14

15

01 An underwater camera records the leaking oil flow from the the *Deepwater Horizon* oil spill, April 2010. Source: BP.
02 Platform supply vessels battle the blazing remnants of the offshore oil rig *Deepwater Horizon*, April 2010. Source: US Coast Guard.
03 An aerial photo shows the gas leak from the offshore gas pipeline Nord Stream 1 in the Baltic Sea. On 26 September 2022, a series of bombings and subsequent underwater gas leaks occurred on the two gas pipelines Nord Stream 1 and Nord Stream 2. Source: Swedish Coast Guard.
04 The gas pipelines of Nord Stream 1 are made of steel that is several centimeters thick and are encapsulated within a layer of concrete. The pipeline runs from Vyborg, in Northwest Russia to Lubmin, Germany, and supplies Western Europe with natural gas. Source: Wikimedia Commons, Vuo.
05 The container ship *Ever Given* stuck in the Suez Canal in Egypt. The incident slowed down global trade significantly in March 2021. Source: NASA JSC ISS image library.
06 A man on an electricity pole, installing an illegal electrical connection in South Africa, 2020. Due to corruption and poor management the country has been dealing with a series of electricity crises for years. On some days, citizens have no power for up to six hours. Source: TikTok, @kwanelesiwa2.
07 A debris that was removed from the International Space Station's cosmic particle detector, 2019. Based on ESA models, the total number of objects in Earth orbit larger than 1 cm in size is likely over one million. Source: NASA library.
08 Collapse of the Reichsbrücke in Vienna, 1 Aug 1976. Photo: Helmut Krcal.
09 A shark bites into an undersea fibre optic internet cable, linking the United States, Europe and Japan.
10 Deforestation in the Brazilian Amazon, state of Rondônia, 2009. Source: Google Earth.
11 The blackout in North and East India on 31 July was the largest power outage in history. A power grid failure, caused by excessive heat waves and high energy demands, affected more than 620 million people (about 9% of the world population). Source: CNN, The Situation Room.
12 Hurricane *Irma* approaches the Leeward Islands at peak intensity on 5 September 2017 as the third most intense Atlantic hurricane on record. Irma caused widespread and catastrophic damage throughout its life-time, particularly in the northeastern Caribbean and the Florida Keys. Source: NOAA.
13 Bombing of an Eni pipeline on the Brass River in Nigeria, 2016. Nigeria is currently losing $ 1.017 million due to recent bombings of pipelines in the Niger Delta.
14 Toilet paper shortage at Tesco during Covid-19, Clonmel, Ireland. March 2020. Source: Flickr, Bernie Goldbach.
15 An image of the Rana Plaza building, one year before its collapse, which occured due to a structural failure on 24 April 2013 in the Savar Upazila of Dhaka District, Bangladesh. The building hosted five garment factories and was declared unsafe several times before it collapsed. Nevertheless, managers send workers into the factories, partially due to the pressure to complete orders from the gobal fashion industry on time. Source: Wikipedia, Sean Robertson.

VISIBLE UPON BREAKDOWN

Exploring the cultural, political and spatial nature of infrastructure

VISIBLE UPON BREAKDOWN

Exploring the cultural, political and spatial nature of infrastructure

Edited by Isabel Seiffert,
Christoph Miler, Justinien Tribillon

Spector Books

JUSTINIEN TRIBILLON

BREAKING DOWN

In-between static poster advertisements the Tokyo subway has rectangular television screens located inside the upper part of the carriages. They broadcast announcements, propaganda, newsreels. The moving images on these screens feed in the cluttered visual and aural landscape typical of Japan's hypermodernity made of bright colours, an accumulation of scripts – kanji, hiragana, katakana, roman – displayed in clashing typefaces, and a heap of sounds and ringtones. It was December 2018. Clutched to a bright orange dangling handle, my whole body was lazily going back and forth as the train accelerated, turned, braked. I was letting my mind roam, imagining that each curve the train took was to avoid conflicting infrastructure – water pipes, gas, sewers – or to go round some plot of real estate Japanese technocrats had failed to secure when the route of the subway network was negotiated. I thought of the *métro* Line 1 in Paris when it reaches Bastille station: it takes a tight bend that can throw you off balance if you don't hold onto something. It does so to avoid the foundations of the July Column erected in celebration of the second French revolution of 1830 – and built where the Bastille Fortress, stormed by the people of Paris on 14 July 1789, stood until its final destruction in 1791. I was cradled by the movements of the carriage when news from France came through on the silent screens in the form of tires set on fire and people wearing high-visibility jackets. The *Gilets jaunes* ("yellow vests")protests had been ignited in November 2018 by a tax increase on petrol

Previous spread: The remains of Genoa's Morandi Bridge are blown up in a controlled explosion, June 2019. Almost a year earlier, on 14 August 2018, during a torrential rainstorm and due to a lack of maintanence, a large section of the bridge collapsed, killing 43 people. When it opened in 1967, Ponte Morandi was one of the longest concrete bridges in the world and a symbol of Italian engineering skills and progress.

perceived as an umpteenth snub from Parisian elites to suburban and rural working classes who had no choice but to use their cars to work, shop, see their friends. Within a few weeks, it had snowballed into an eclectic national protest that dragged many social and political issues in its nets, but mainly focused on the cost of living and spatial inequality. The protests had used roundabouts as their rallying points and the high-vis jackets that all drivers must carry in their cars as their iconic garment. Roundabouts are a ubiquitous element of road design in France – it is said the country holds the world record for its numbers (65,127 in 2021) – and it seemed their central islets, often endowed with "public art" or shrubberies made the ideal grounds for protest camps. The traffic calming device had now been transformed to host a "road rage" of a new kind. The movement was omnipresent in French news, but I was surprised to see it had followed me to Japan. In hindsight I suppose it ticked many boxes of global newsworthiness: it fit the cliché of the riotous French that is loved by both French nationals and foreigners, it was very graphic (fires, violence, destruction, striking symbols), and it touched on issues that working-classes and lower middle-classes could relate to worldwide. Finally, its setting – road infrastructure – was a technological landscape familiar to many.

Fast forward to February 2022. As I wrote the first version of this text, the Ambassador Bridge that connects Ontario to Detroit had just been "reclaimed" by Canadian officials after being blocked for nearly a week by anti-vaccine protestors who created logjams across the country using lorries and cars, blocking essential international trade. In Europe, the so-called Freedom Convoys, inspired by Canada's truckers, were headed to Brussels to express their anger by gridlocking the unofficial capital city of the European Union. The reclaiming of the road as a protest ground by those who most use it, the sabotaging of speed, the clogging of motorways, are dramatic and desperate expressions of anger from those who present themselves as the "people *from below*" against those "above". When striking consists in stopping work and blocking access to one's workstation in an effort to pressure the bosses' coffers, protests like the Gilets jaunes and the Freedom convoys consist in symbolic occupations of the one space that remains an essential expression of modernity – the road – using its most iconic vehicle: the car. Beyond its cultural impact, sabotaging roads guarantees the disruption of international fluxes of goods and produce that are critical to the normal functioning of capitalist economies.

The protest movements of the Gilet jaunes (2018–2019) and the Freedom convoys (2022) illustrate some fundamental aspects of the concept of infrastructure at the core of this curatorial and editorial project. Without the Ambassador Bridge blockade, or the Suez Canal blockage in March 2021 (a human error), you probably would not have considered those allegorical pipes made of concrete, steel, working men and women, administrative constraints, practice, that allow our global interconnected capitalist economies to "perform". They remain invisible to the many until they *break down*. Secondly, these dramatic events reveal the dual nature of infrastructure – the concrete and the metaphorical.

A blocked road is impressive because we associate it with speed, passage, and communication – and we are struck by the incompatibility of an infrastructure designed for communication that is now stuck. A blocked road becomes even more frightening when you realise that it is not only a symbol reclaimed by a group whose struggle you are more or less sympathetic with, but that through this conduit passes produce, automobile parts, clothes, toys, chips for your electronics, electricity, internet, etc. Those invisible layers that also constitute the foundations of your lifestyle are thus chipped away, becoming an inexpungable source of stress. In a series of academic articles published at the end of the 1990s, the American anthropologist Susan Star offered a series of defining elements for the concept of infrastructure.[1] Among them, that they become *visible upon breakdown*. The phrase has inspired the curatorial exploration of this project: delving into the concept of infrastructure by way of photography.

The project "Visible upon breakdown" was initially designed as an exhibition, scheduled for the 2020 and then 2021 editions of the Arles Photography Festival, cancelled twice because of Covid. Inspired by social sciences' approach to infrastructure, the exhibition was organised in three conceptual chapters that would have enabled the visitors to delve into several layers of infrastructure: "origins", from the collapse of the Morandi bridge to commodification; "power and politics", that looked at the landscape of finance and the militarisation of the Swiss mountains, to a final part: "psyches of infrastructure", that dived into the cracks of the Earth and those of our minds.

After the second cancellation of our exhibition in Arles, Christoph Miler, Isabel Seiffert (who together form Offshore) and I promised ourselves and the photographers we had brought into this adventure that this project we had developed since 2018 would not just die away. The world's reaction to Covid had just created the most formidable and tragic breakdown our societies had known for decades, bringing under the spotlight the essential fluxes, infrastructures of care and "essential workers" that would be forgotten once again as soon as everything went back to "normal". "Visible upon breakdown" felt more important than ever. May it be Covid-19, cancer, or other absolute challenges to existence, this project also collided for us with the fight for one's life that surprises you when you least expect it. To complete it today in the form of a book is a celebration of the extraordinary survivors whose exceptional strength and love of life inspire us, always.

In our collaboration with the team in Arles – Sam Stourdzé, Caroline Courrioux, Amélie Samson, Christoph Wiesner – we had worked hard not to create a book, but an exhibition. Offshore being art directors and designers with great experience in printed matter, myself an editor and writer – together, co-creators of the print periodical *Migrant Journal* – Arles was meant

1 Susan Leigh Star, 'The Ethnography of Infrastructure', *American Behavioral Scientist* 43, no. 3 (1999), 377–91.

to be our first major exhibition as curators. We had worked hard to show the Arles team that had awarded us a curatorial grant in 2019 that we were keen to get out of our comfort zone, eager to propose an exhibition and not a book whose pages we would have metaphorically torn off to placate on walls. As a demonstration of our commitment to this new medium for us, and to channel our energy, we had also decided not to publish a "catalogue". The text to accompany the photographers' projects was minimal, to let photography speaks for itself.

Disheartened by a second cancellation – we had just finished redesigning the exhibition for a third venue, we were days away from the press conference and entering the production phase – and aware Covid had created a backlog of exhibitions that would take several years to clear, we decided to refocus and rework the project as ink and pulp. This journey took three extra years.

In the coming pages, we feature the works of seven photographers. From Singapore to Lausanne, Kiruna to Masdar, the Netherlands to Kenya, their projects strip layer after layer off infrastructure. The effects of mining, land-reclaiming, tree-planting, bank-storming, bunkering, and automating are dissected to offer multimedia, visual-dominated sets of evidence that enrich our understanding of structural networks. But we also wanted to add an extra layer of intellectual infrastructure and commissioned three thinkers to write original essays on how their ongoing research connects with the concept of infrastructure. Charlotte Malterre-Barthes (page 130) on non-extractive architecture, Armelle Choplin (page 68) on concrete with a focus on West Africa, and Gabriella Garcia on sex work and digital infrastructure (page 194). I have also contributed an essay on the mysterious origins of the concepts of infrastructure (page 262). The brief was not to produce critiques of the visual projects that are published in this book, for we wanted to allow unfiltered access to the photographic works thta are of great density and can fend for themselves. Instead, the essays bring another dimension through another medium – writing and reading – completing the transformation of this curatorial project into a book.

SIM CHI

SHIFTING

12

YIN

SANDS

13

[DE/NEO/POST]COLONIALISM ARCHITECTURAL FETISHISM CHINA COLLAPSE COMMODIFIED NATURE CONCRETE EXTRACTION EROSION FINANCIAL FLUXES MALAYSIA PERIPHERIES PERSECUTION OF INDIGENOUS COMMUNITIES PETROL CULTURE REAL ESTATE RECLAMATION SAND TRAFFICKING VIETNAM

This loose granular substance most of us will associate with beaches, beauty, and leisure is, with gravel, the most extracted material worldwide: sand. As the main component of concrete, sand constitutes the foundation of our rapid urban expansion. But sand is disappearing fast. Its traffic, legal or criminal, illustrates a near-caricatural relationship between the planet's wealthiest and poorest communities. As it shifts across space, commodified, the overexploitation of this shared resource generates tremendous social, economic, and ecological violence. In 2017, Singapore was the largest importer of sand according to the United Nations. This country of 5 million inhabitants, living on a territory the size of New York City, has increased its surface area by 23 per cent since 1963.

In “Shifting Sands”, an ongoing project started in 2017, Sim Chi Yin initially questioned the sand addiction in her home country of Singapore, before extending her research scope to Malaysia, Vietnam, and China. She focused specifically on “land reclamation”, a process that describes the creation of new lands from water by discharging immense quantities of matter —cement, gravels, and sand—in oceans, wetlands, lakes and riverbeds. Could it be that our absurd, greedy, self-destructive relationship to natural resources is best encapsulated by the concept of land reclamation? When we “reclaim” land on the sea to, eventually, sell it. With “Shifting Sands”, Sim asks who is “reclaiming”? For whom? And from whom?

In Vietnam, Sim Chi Yin's photographs also document the erosion and the aftermath of landslides in the Mekong Delta, where the lives of communities that have lived harmoniously with their environment for centuries are now threatened by large-scale sand mining. In mixing bird's-eye-view shots made with drones, with human-scale photographs, and a new 10-minute virtual reality piece, the artist plays with the points of view and aesthetics that condition our relationship to the Earth and the impact of the overexploitation of its resources.

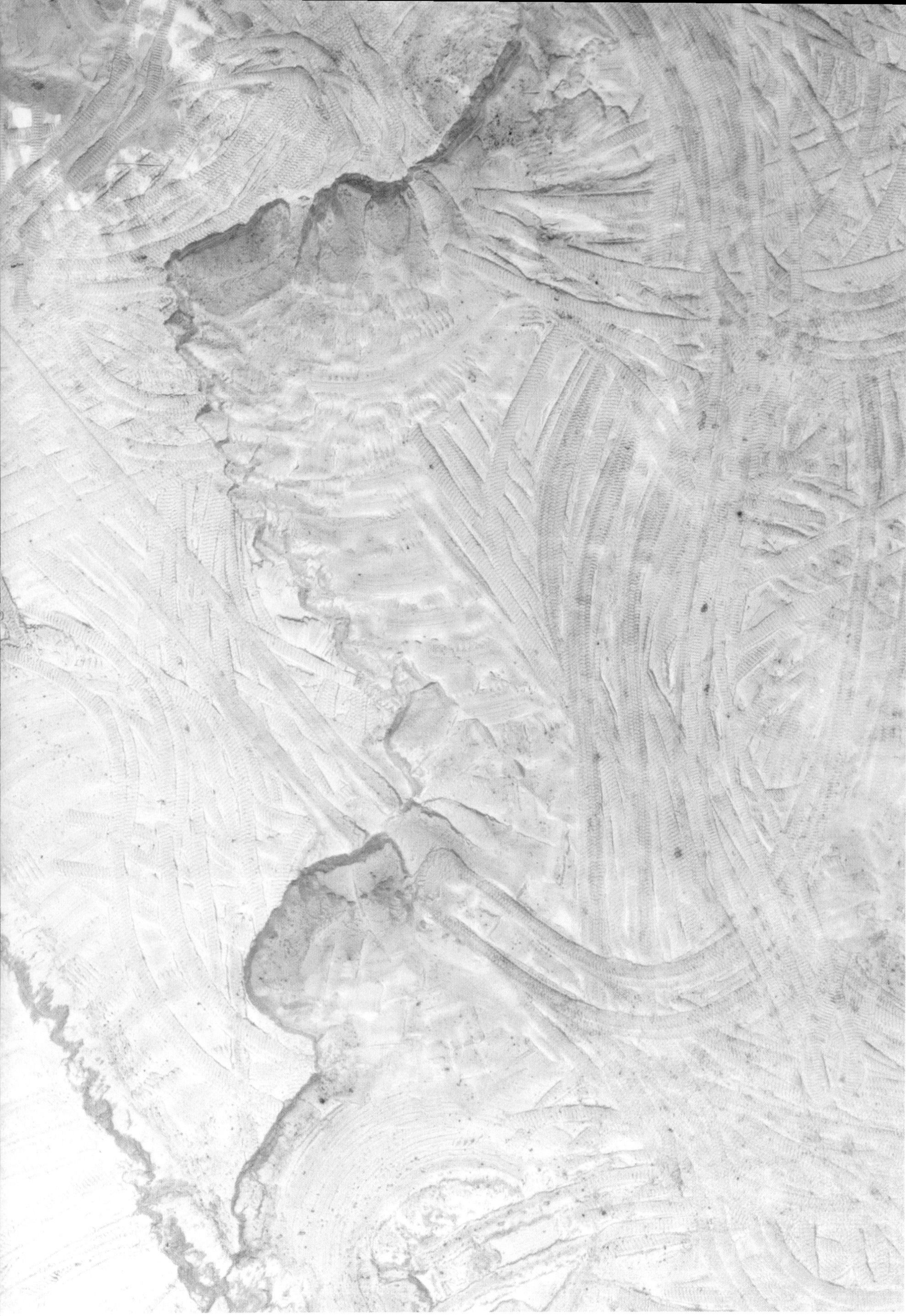

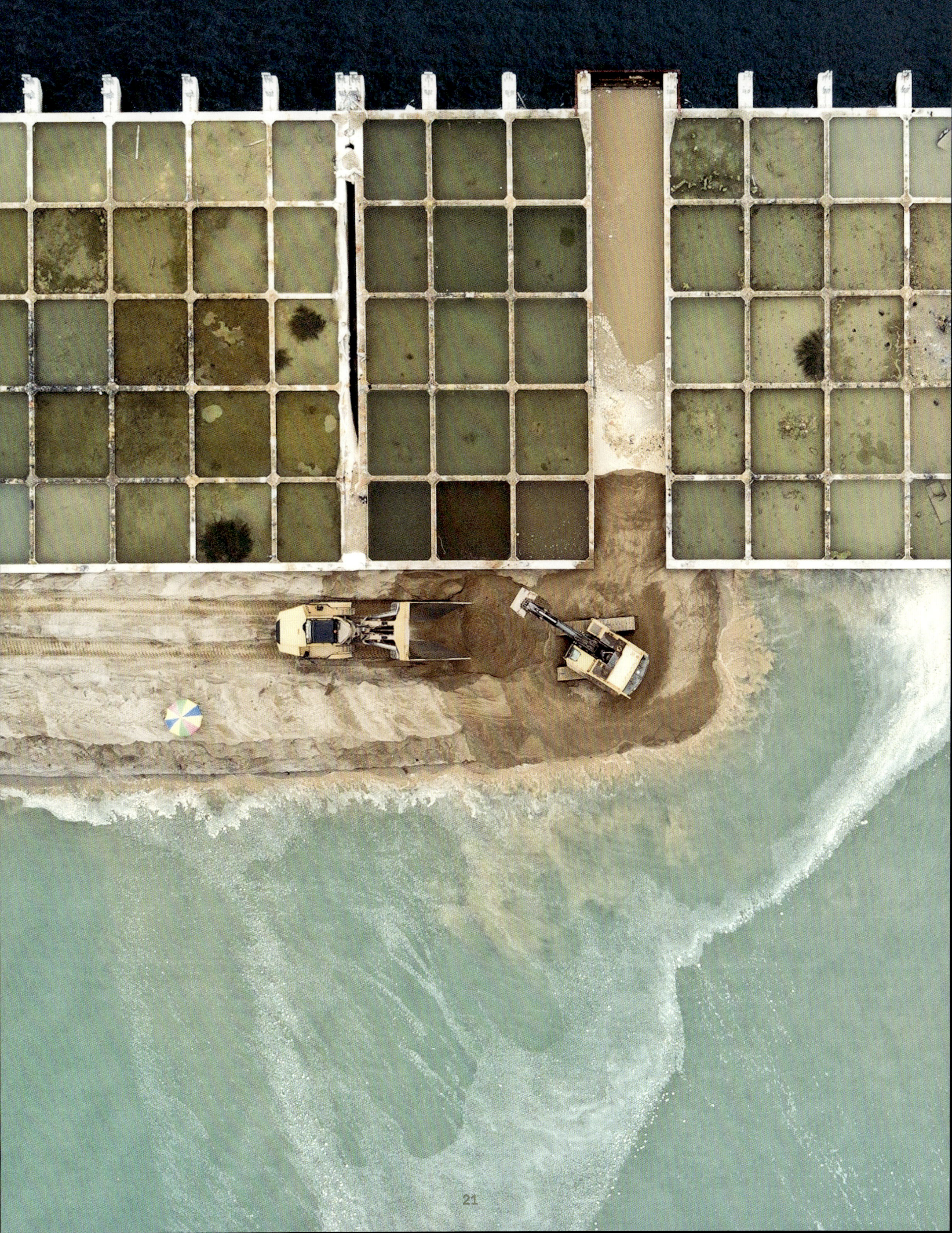

01

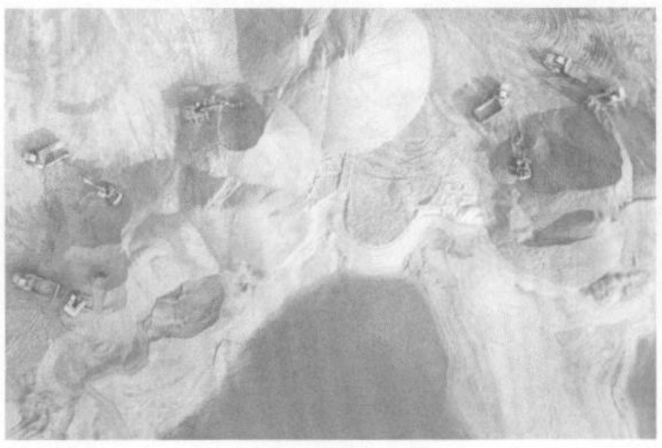

02

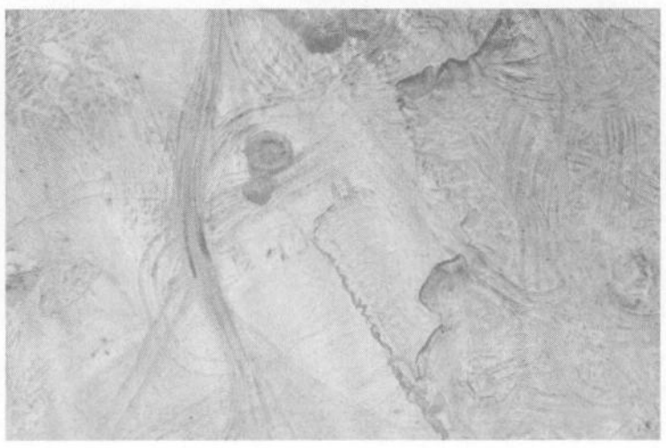

03

04

01 One of four artificial islands being build in the sea off a coast of Johor in southern Malaysia, part of a mega development named—with no irony intended—"Forest City".

02 A drone shot of a bank of sand surcharge used in a massive reclamation project being done around Singapore's new port in Tuas, the country's westernmost area. The first phase of the 30-year project will go into use by the early 2020s and it will eventually become the largest single container terminal in the world. In the on-going first phase of construction alone, 294 hectares of land are being reclaimed. Sand, due to its porous nature is used to cover and weigh down on reclamation fill material in order to compact it and remove pressure from water trapped within. Of the some 100 cubic metres of reclamation fill material required for the current pier being built—the second of what will eventually be four piers—70 per cent will be from material dredged from the seabed or excavated from other local infrastructure projects like subway tunnelling.

03 Four caissons (watertight retaining structures) sit off the coast of Tuas, awaiting use to reclaim a huge piece of land for the country's new container port terminal. They are temporarily stored here, near a long white structure stretching out to sea—a series of joined caissons which will form a retaining wall for one of pier structures where ships will dock.

04 Land reclamation works in Tuas. Singapore has been short of sand for its sizeable and continual land reclamation and construction work, having bought sand from its neighbouring Southeast Asian countries for decades.

05

06

07

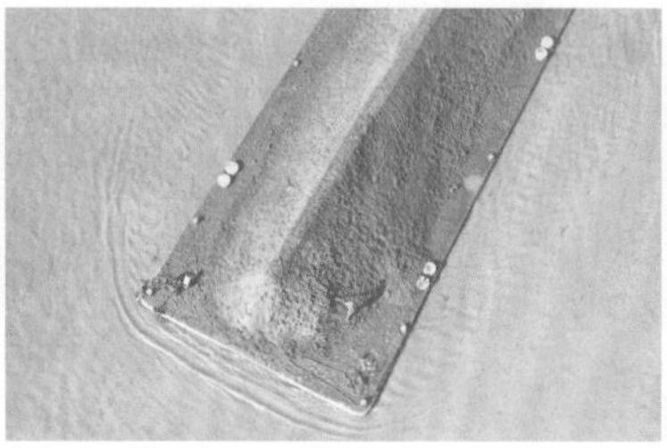

08

09

10

11

12

05 A flotilla of sand barges wait to unload their mounds of sand in the straits between Singapore and Malaysia. They are depositing their loads at the Forest City development—a joint venture between a China developer with the state government and Sultan of Johor. The ambitious project plans to create four artificial islands out of the sea. One has so far been completed, with a hotel, residential and commercial complex built on it. It is being presented as a development that is green and a model of future urban planning, but has displaced aboriginals and disrupted traditional fishing grounds and eco life.

06 Nguyen Thi Hong, 45, who runs a small cafe, returns to her house destroyed by erosion, a week after the midnight landslide struck (28 June 2017). Hers was among five houses that partially fell into the river in this commune of Hiep Phuoc, in Nha Be district, 33 kilometre southeast of Saigon. Parts of the Mekong Delta are eroding at rates alarming to experts who say it is caused by on-going damming work and rampant sand dredging upstream in the Mekong River. Vietnam, like many other countries around the world, is starting to feel the environmental and social costs of large-scale sand mining.

07 A very overloaded sand barge in the Mekong Delta, transporting sand dredged up from the the Mekong. Vietnam's sand is consumed locally but also exported to countries like Singapore.

08 On Chau Ma island in the Mekong Delta, farmers harvest and grind amaranth. Some of them are now landless as river-bank erosion has swept away their ancestral farmland. The island, which used to have 5,000 inhabitants, has lost about half of its land and people have moved away.

09 A reservoir being constructed in Lanzhou New Area in China's west—a new city built out of a desert landscape.

10 A stockpile of sand in Bedok, eastern Singapore, as seen from a public road. This reserve, which belongs to the country's main building authority—the Housing and Development Board—is ringed by two layers of fencing. Land-scarce Singapore, which has reclaimed about 20 per cent of its area since becoming an independent country in 1965, has had a long history of creating land out of the sea and swamps since British colonial times in the 1820s. It flattened many of its hills and ran out of its own supply of sand decades ago and has been buying sand from its Southeast Asian neighbours for reclamation and construction work. This stockpile has sand and gravel.

11 A family takes a walk and goes fishing in an area in southern Malaysia now covered with giant sand dunes. The Danga Bay area is earmarked for a massive residency and commercial development, with much of the land reclaimed. Mangroves nearby appear to have been drowned by sand. The world is running out of sand as Asia's rapid urbanisation is driving up demand like never before.

12 A sand hill behind hoarding, on a construction site on Fort Road, Singapore.

ETIENNE I

THE CITY

38

IALAPERT

OF POSSI

39

EBILITIES

40

[DE/NEO/POST]COLONIALISM ARCHITECTURAL FETISHISM CONNECTED OBJECTS CONSUMERIST DESIRE GERMANY FOSSIL FUEL LUST PETROL CULTURE RECLAMATION RETROFITTING SAND TECHNOSOLUTIONISM TIRED BODIES UNITED ARAB EMIRATES

Masdar is an ecotopia in the desert, where pale golden sand has replaced luxuriant green. A dystopian "smart" city in Abu Dhabi boasting full carbon neutrality. Its Wikipedia page rings as the bingo of sustainable capitalism—by all means, an oxymoron—or a wish list to a Santa Claus wearing the shemagh of the local aristocracy and the turtleneck of Norman Foster, the city's architect. Its poetic name, *madinat masdar*, translates as the "source city" and evokes the Origin, the Earth and its ancient sediments while the actual design of Masdar displays layers over layers of sociotechnical imaginaries. The source of black gold, the precious oil, is drying out and with it the country's safe horizon. The city is the expression of petrodollars for a green future, Emirati fantasies of technological tomorrows and yesterday's traditions, a sandbox for German industrial giants and British starchitects.

In 2006, it was announced it would take eight years to build. Now its delivery date has been pushed to 2030. But the brand-new city of six square kilometres—whose initial renders look more like a Roman castrum in the desert than a 21st-century city—slowly breaks ground on new buildings, hosting its first inhabitants, offices, and universities.

In 2015, French photographer Etienne Malapert arrived in Masdar with his view camera to capture the *source*. Stormy landscapes and shiny sportscars, vents and fences, back entrances and servant quarters, content citizens and harassed workers. Malapert captures the ambition and contradiction of Masdar, the architecture and the people, without caustic prejudice nor mellowing fascination. He offers his take on a city that has come before the society it is meant to support. The first green ghost town?

NOTICE
KEEP GATE CLOSED AT ALL TIMES
NOTICE
KEEP GATE CLOSED AT ALL TIMES
NOTICE
AUTHORISED PERSONNEL ONLY
محطة
الطاقة الشمسية
10 MW SOLAR PANEL FARM

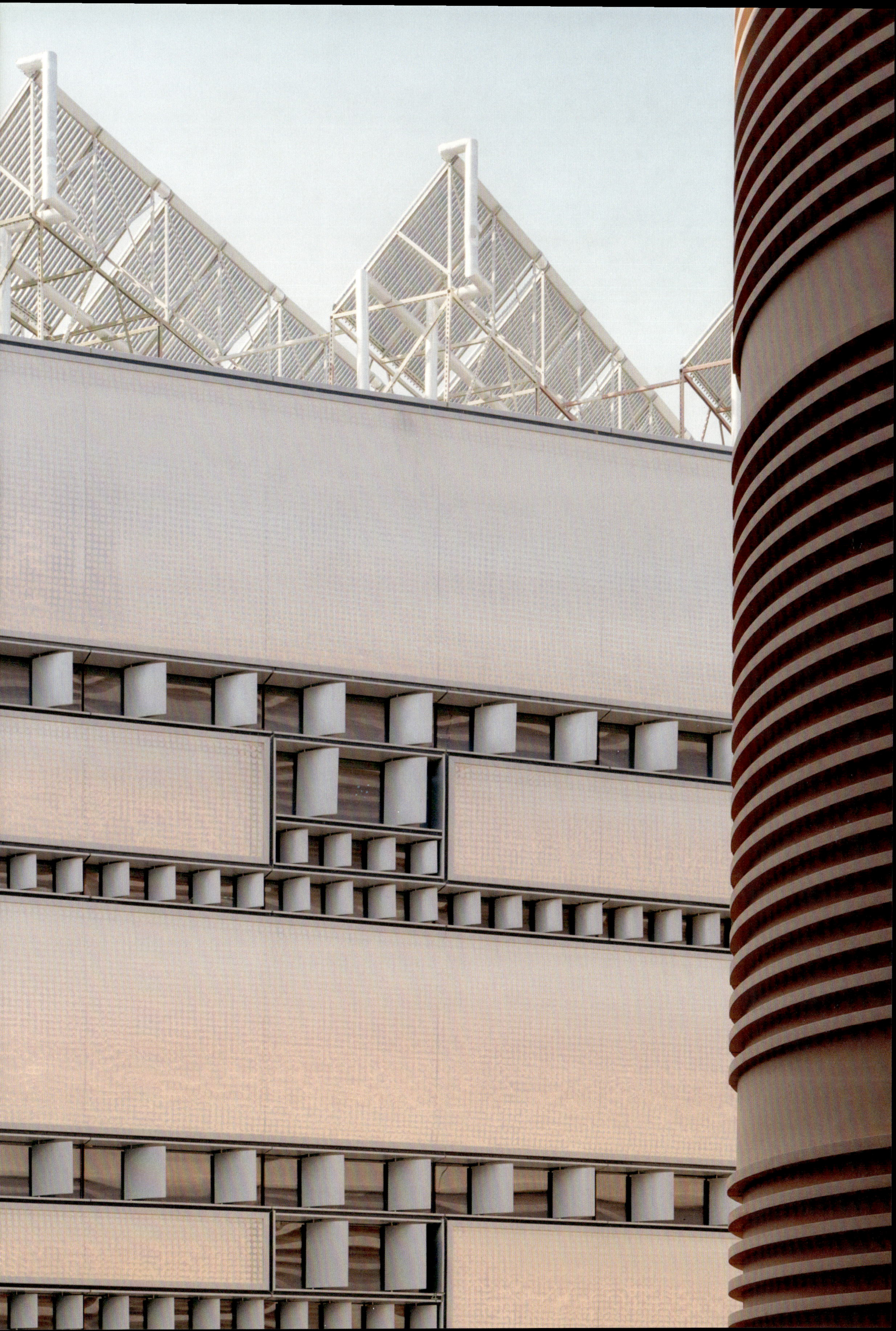

53
82776

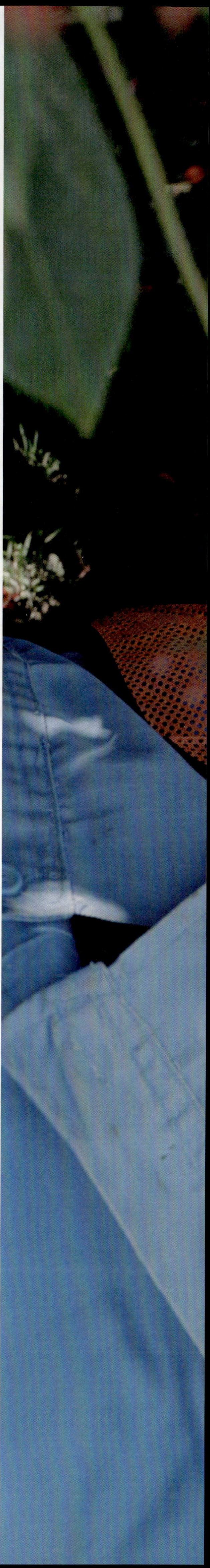

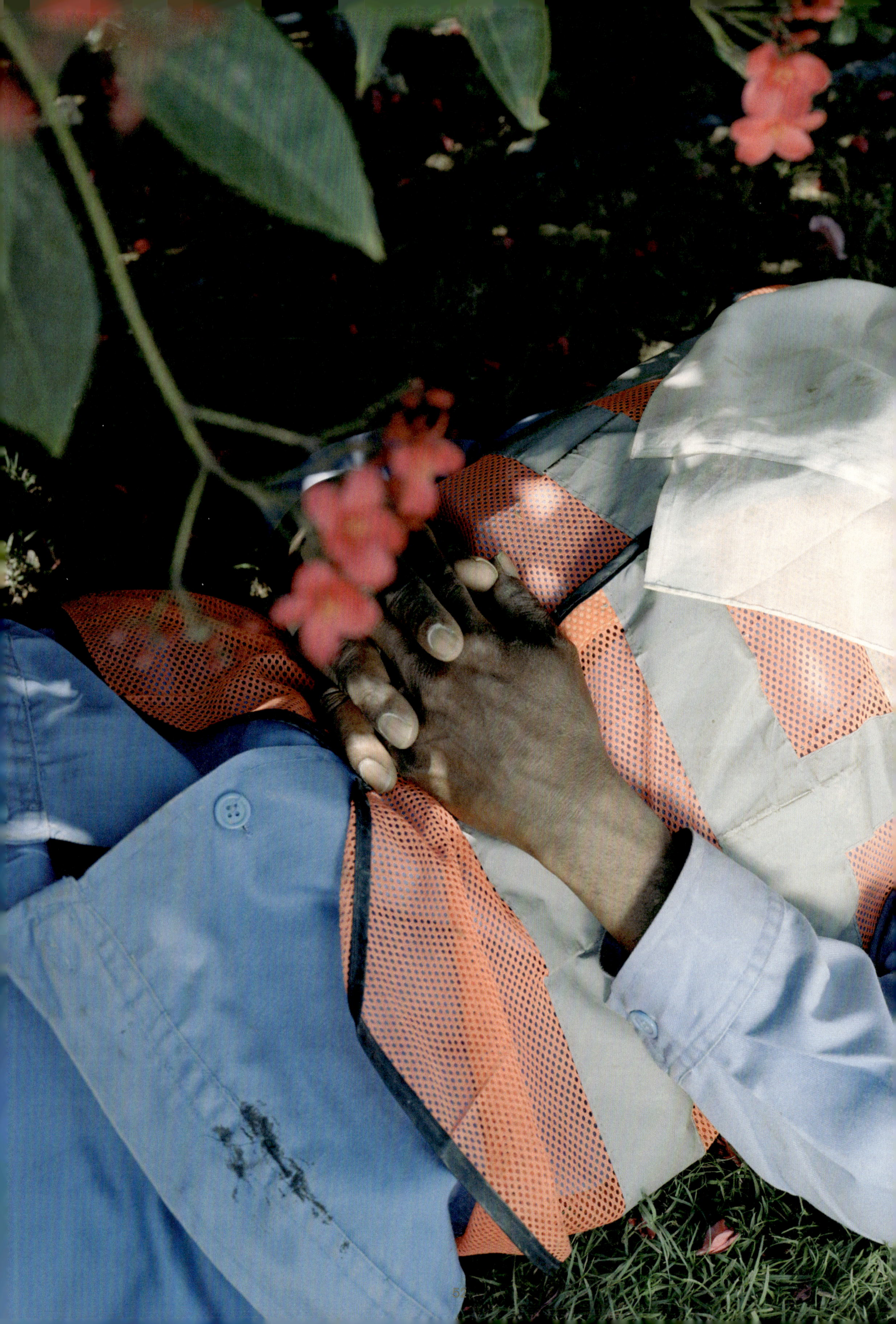

RIGMAN®
SAFETY

TANK CAPACITY
2.1M3
BRIDGESTONE

Club Car

01

02

03

04

01 Once I get there, I am faced with some serious difficulties: four-metre high wire fences, CCTV cameras and signs stating that it is "strictly prohibited to enter without authorisation". I quickly glance around the place but cannot see anyone even though a small door is open. I take the risk.

02 Tahra offers to make me visit other beautiful places. I follow her. Unfortunately, I am already familiar with all these places. I think I do not need her anymore, and I tell her I would email her if I need her help again. In order to mark the occasion, I offer to take her picture with the large format camera in the middle of the desert.

03 I try to reach the rooftop to get a different point of view. After having climbed ten floors on foot—and under the sun—I open the door leading to the roof. I look down and I see a strange empty square made by barriers in a middle of nowhere.

04 As the small electric cars from yesterday are still driving around in my mind, I wonder about the electric supply and production in Masdar. I know that there is a big field of solar panels and plants on the outskirts of town—not far away from where I am. This is probably where a big part of the energy supply is produced. I have found my morning's mission.

05

06

07

08

09

09

10

12

05 Everything looks so perfect, and yet so strange to the European eye. I decide to have a walk around in order to discover more about this place and what is going on here. With eyes wide open in order to admire the buildings' facades and the solar panels on the roofs, I wonder about the usefulness of many architectural items.

06 Once I have arrived in Masdar, I soon realise that what I considered to be a sandstorm in Abu Dhabi is nothing compared to what it is here. It is hard to walk against the wind, I can hardly open my eyes and breathing has become a physical challenge.

07 I go down the huge spiral staircase in the information building, overlooked by three paintings depicting the sheikh Khalifa bin Zayed Al-Nahyan and previous sheikhs.

08 The first facade is beige with a wrought iron doorway lit up by two little wall lamps just as elaborate as the entrance. Parked in front of this little villa, I see what resembles a game of Tetris—three super-cars: a Corvette, a Porsche and a Mustang.

09 They decide to take a nap under the trees of the beautiful villas, like they usually do after lunch. They lie down, each one under a different flowery tree, and they lay their head on a piece of wood. Since I really get along with them, I decide to stay and enjoy a bit of shade to catch up on my lack of sleep.

10 I see the car approaching with a shrill whistle. The vehicle or PRT (Personal Rapid Transit) stops in parking space number one. A group of German people get off. It is my turn now. Once I am sitting on the leather seat, a voice invites me to put my finger on a little touch screen to start the car. Without cables or rails, it takes me through underground corridors until we reach the basement of the research centre, the Masdar Institute.

11 After a long day of work, I'm waiting for the bus to go back to Abu Dhabi. Next to the bus station, I see a solar panel covered by trees. I step forward to take a closer look. I then laugh as the sun cannot reach the panel because there are too many leaves.

12 All the furniture is white, impersonal. It looks like a clinic or a sterilisation centre. We head towards the basement where the research labs are situated. At the end of a hallway, a strong blue light is projected onto the ground.

13 The tower itself is very hard to photograph because it is too high and I cannot move further away. I will take one from

13

14

15

16

17

18

19

the other side of the railings. There are so many interesting things here: mirrors, solar panels seen from underneath, and all the other facilities.

14 I had come across small vehicles provided with 100 per cent electric motors on the Internet, but I would not have thought they would come that far from the city centre. Indeed, this is not one of these electric cars, but a golf buggy that appears, driven by a man dressed like a parking valet who offers to drive me to the other side of the parking lot, i.e. 50 metres away.

15 I had not thought it would take me a full 45 minutes to cross the desert in order to get to the city. Fortunately, there are stones amidst the sand—I would have been much slower otherwise. Staring at the ground, I walk on, obsessed with the idea of a cold bottle of Coke. Despite my longing for some coolness and shade, I stop to take some pictures of the landscape. I can see Masdar far away, bathed in a beautiful, orangey blue light.

16 The light starts to dim. It is already 5.30 pm. I cross the parking lot towards the bus stops with the same question still in mind. I then meet an Emirati who is also waiting for the bus but we don't share a language. I point at my camera to get him to understand that I would like to take a picture of him. He agrees. I end the day with this man's portrait.

17 I am a bit sceptical: although it looks very impressive, the field of solar panels is not really photogenic. Nevertheless, I try to capture this place to the best of my ability. Finally, one last camera angle behind the wire fences seems to do the trick.

18 Everything looks so different when there is no landmark—no horizon, no sky, no ground. This atmosphere will allow me to take more abstract photos. I do not really know where to look. But I think some abstraction provoked by a climate disruption will bring something interesting to this project.

19 They invite me to drink tea with them. From behind a wall, they bring out everything one needs to prepare tea: a tea pot, some cups, some milk and sugar, and some spoons. One of them pours me a cup of tea. It has nothing to do with the idea I had of a tea preparation in the Middle East: it is a proper English tea. I want to make the most of every opportunity and I ask if I can take a group portrait. Only two of them accept.

ARMELLE CHOPLIN

HEART OF CONCRETENESS

Once upon a time there was an old mother pig who had three little pigs and not enough food to feed them. So when they were old enough, she sent them out into the world to seek their fortunes. The first little pig was very lazy. He didn't want to work at all and he built his house out of straw. The second little pig worked a little bit harder but he was somewhat lazy too and he built his house out of sticks. Then, they sang and danced and played together the rest of the day. The third little pig worked hard all day and built his house with bricks and cement. It was a sturdy house complete with a fine fireplace and chimney. It looked like it could withstand the strongest winds.

Emblematic of frenetic capitalistic urban development, concrete is a pervasive material shaping contemporary landscapes and societies. Concrete stands and circulates at the heart of major financial investments, political powers, and environmental debates. Concrete epitomises the contradictions of our societies. Digging deep and building high. Extraction, construction and very often destruction. Holes to extract the sand, gravel, and cement to make concrete to build towers. The Swiss mountains drilled by quarries. The cement plants of Nigeria feeding Lagos's sprawl. The cracked earth of Kiruna, a mining town in the far north of Sweden. The Mekong Delta in Vietnam melting away in the river. This is the topography of our world of concrete.

Denounced as a "weapon of mass construction of capitalism" by the philosopher Anselm Jappe, ardently defended and lauded by the architect Rudy Ricciotti, or presented as a solution to poverty by the World Bank, concrete fuels controversies. Since the invention of Portland cement in the 19th century, concrete – a mixture of cement, aggregates (sand or gravel) and water–has become a global phenomenon. Symbol of modernity that had its heyday in the 1960s, concrete is the material that has accompanied the accelerated urbanisation of the world since the Second World War. Concrete is now the world's leading material in terms of volume produced and consumed, ahead of steel and plastic. As a result of this global success, the cement industry is responsible for 8 per cent of annual greenhouse gas emissions. Concrete is under attack and construction companies are denounced as polluters. The shift is brutal, since only yesterday they were presented as the national pride and flagship of the economy. In Switzerland, during the autumn of 2020, environmental activists set up on Mormont Hill exploited by LafargeHolcim. The first Swiss ZAD (*Zone à Défendre*, Area to defend) was created to denounce the extension of the quarry. At the same time, Extinction Rebellion activists were invading concrete stations in the Greater Paris area to block the construction of several new transport infrastructures across the region. But in the Global South, the demand for concrete is growing. It has come to symbolise values of modernity and success, and has redefined social practices, forms of dwelling, and popular imaginaries.

THE LAST FRONTIERS OF CEMENT

Cities of emerging countries are the new frontiers of grey gold. Cement consumption is now used as an index of development, often compared to GDP. The world average is around 500 kilogramme per capita. In West Africa, the ratio is barely over 100 kilogramme. The market is promising, and the major European cement companies, such as Franco-Swiss LafargeHolcim and German Heidelberg, have understood this. But they are now being challenged by Nigerian Aliko Dangote, Africa's biggest fortune and the world's 25th largest. This cement magnate embodies the new figure of success and “Africapitalism”, a trend driven by African businessmen who claim to be philanthropists and aim first and foremost at the development of their continent. Cement, which was once associated with the colonists who imported it, is now presented as a 100 per cent African product. In the streets of West African cities like Lagos, Cotonou, and Lomé it is possible to buy bags of cement at any hour, night or day. Main roads are equipped with hardware stores selling cement, steel reinforcing bars, piles of gravel, and sand. Cement and concrete are everywhere: both on the cranes that build so-called modern towers in the city centres, and in the distant suburbs where poor households incrementally construct their homes. The pervasive grey colour of concrete offers a regular reminder that the city is constantly under construction, and that no one is exempt from dealing with cement. Rich and poor, decision-makers and ordinary urbanites: everyone has something to say about this material of great banality. The price per ton is chalked up every day on the shop fronts, like the price on the local stock exchange.

In Abidjan, a 12-year-old boy told me that he would like to become rich and famous, and hesitated between becoming a footballer, like Didier Drogba, or a cement seller, like Aliko Dangote.

From Eko Atlantic City, the artificial island in the heart of Lagos, to the outskirts of Dakar, to the new city of Diamniadio or Akon City, created by the famous Senegalese-American singer and named after himself, futuristic concrete towers are constantly being built. Bridges, bypasses, and “social” housing programmes are being launched in West African cities such as Abidjan, Accra and Cotonou, at a cost of millions of dollars but also, and above all, tons of concrete (and of sand and gravel). As a symbol of economic emergence, a consensus has been reached on this material, as it is both a source of enrichment for the wealthy and a promise of a better life for the poorest.

A LIVING MATERIAL

In French-speaking West Africa, the children learn to read and write with *Mamadou and Bineta’s Book of reading French for African schools*.[1] Lesson 55 is entitled “The beautiful houses in my village”: “In my village, there are not only huts: there are also beautiful and solid houses whose walls are built with bricks and cement and whose roofs are covered with tiles or corrugated iron”. The pupils are then invited to copy and memorise the new words: bricks, cement, tiles and corrugated iron. Concrete houses are “naturally” beautiful.

Concrete is an affectively charged material. Behind this inert material, there is life, lives, and the hopes of millions of men and women who seek to shelter their loved ones. In the Global South where social security is inexistent and access to the banking system is difficult, buying bags of cement, investing in concrete is a way of hoarding. In the shanty towns in particular, building in concrete makes it possible to legitimise one’s presence, to break away from the precariousness of wood and sheet metal, and to no longer be at the mercy of eviction policies and floods. Cement becomes a product of first necessity and the concrete block materialises the "right to the city" and one's belonging to it.

Unlike its production, which requires a very advanced and energy-consuming technology, cement is simple to use. Mixing it does not require a steady electrical power source nor does it require formal training or literacy. Pictograms on the bags sold are there to remind people of the proportions, which are known to everyone, including women. Many of them build by themselves to have their own house and no longer suffer from the family yoke. For them, concrete becomes a symbol of emancipation. Concrete is nevertheless a symbol of virility, as the emblems of the cement manufacturers' brands (elephant, buffalo, shield, eagle, cuirassier) remind us. The success of individuals is measured by the tons of concrete they have poured. "For a retirement, we offer the teachers two tons of cement. It's a sign of recognition and success," explains a university colleague in Cotonou, Benin. And in West Africa, lovers offer each other bags of cement as a declaration of love, as a "durable" proof of their commitment to each other.

UNINHABITABLE WORLD

But in the context of global environmental change, concrete means heat islands, soil impermeability and mandatory air conditioning. It also means limestone extraction, massive sand removal, release of harmful particles, rubble, and ruins. Concrete is ecologically unsustainable and does not age well. Several tragedies remind us of its obsolescence especially when it is reinforced with corrodible steel: the collapse of the Morandi bridge in Genoa in 2018 killing 43, the fall of a balcony in Angers (France) in 2016 killing 4 young people and injuring 14 others, the destruction of the Ikoyi tower in Lagos in 2021 killing 40 individuals. These tragedies herald the end of the concrete era. They question the choice of construction materials, their environmental footprint, and their maintenance, which is lacking in many cities due to insufficient financial resources or political will. The obsolescent concrete is creating an uninhabitable world.

In *Species of Space*, Georges Perec, qualifies some spaces as "Uninhabitable". Among those feature "the vainglorious mediocrity of tower blocks", the "shanty towns, townships", the "hostile, the grey, the anonymous…" we could add François's concrete house to the list of "uninhabitable spaces". I met François in Cotonou, the economic capital of Benin. I had come to visit him and see his new house, located on the outskirts. He told me how happy he was to see his sacrifices bear fruit in the form of a home. But he also confessed to one of his home's major flaws: "the problem is that it is too hot inside. At night, I get up to sleep outside because it's too hot for me. But outside, there are the mosquitoes." François has built an uninhabitable house. Many people across West Africa report that they often sleep badly because of the intolerable heat accentuated by concrete.

1 *Les Premières lectures de Mamadou et Bineta. Livre de lecture et de français à l'usage des écoles africaines.* Written by Alain Davesne. First edition in 1934. Latest edition in 1996.

This is definitively not a material adapted to the tropical climate. It requires the use of air-conditioning which is energy-intensive and increases the carbon footprint. "Cooling" makes our concrete cities habitable while at the same time making the planet uninhabitable. The circle is vicious. It invites us to rethink the "habitability" of the planet with the Cameroonian philosopher and historian Achille Mbembe. In his 2020 book *Brutalisme*, he suggests that "it is on the African continent, the birthplace of humanity, that the question of the earth will now be posed in the most unexpected, the most complex and the most paradoxical way. It is here, indeed, that the possibilities of decay are most glaring. But it is also here that the opportunities for creative metastasis are the most mature."

GREEN EXPECTATIONS

Alternatives proposing a more rational use of concrete are being explored. More and more architects and engineers want to do away with all-concrete construction. Some advocate the reuse of materials, the recycling of stone and building site waste to promote the circular economy in the construction industry. Experiments conducted by the CRAterre research centre in Grenoble or the Fact Sahel+ collective in Sahelian countries are promoting constructions with recognised thermal values, vernacular know-how or the use of local materials, such as straw, earth, bamboo or typha reed. Research is being carried out on urban metabolism to better understand the life cycle of construction materials. The Polytechnic Schools of Lausanne and Zurich, via the Sustainable Construction Chair, are working on the development of "decarbonised" concrete.
In her 2019 essay, *Nos Cabanes* ("Our wood cabins"), Marielle Macé suggests to re-examine the world through a lighter form of inhabiting. Building a cabin could be a first step towards a larger project that seeks to reinvent collective forms of living together. Macé proposes to move away from our societies of bunkers and concrete, which favour individualism, to build together the foundations of a more worthwhile and sustainable society. Her work reminds us that Le Corbusier did not finish his life in the concrete buildings he built in Switzerland and across Europe but in a wooden hut, "Le Cabanon", by the sea on the French Riviera… In the uninhabitable concrete world that we are shaping, we may be forced to abandon our concrete towers and cities to live in the holes we have dug.

OFFSHORE

ME WEISS

74

WAS CHA

75

PASSIERE

76

ANXIETY CONCRETE FEAR LOCKDOWN RECLAMATION RÉDUIT NATIONAL RETROFITTING SELF-HELP SWITZERLAND WEAPONISED LANDSCAPE

The mountains of Switzerland stand tall, iconic and protective. Their crests and crevasses embody layers upon layers of Swiss nationhood, from rocks to myths, glaciers to nougat. The stylised triangular shape of the Matterhorn exists in golden-packaged chocolate and almond bits in airports around the world while the representations of its bright green prairies, wood beam chalets and misty mornings have become the quintessence of mountainous landscape, wild and pure—and, incidentally, of humankind's domination of a hostile nature. But the core of Swiss identity, the mountains of Switzerland have also been modified as a passive and proactive infrastructure of defence against external enemies. Their caverns are bunkers while fake rocks dissimulate canons.

From the late 19th century and up until a few years ago, the Swiss army had designed a defence strategy named Réduit national that militarised its idyllic landscape to prevent any foreign invasions. Battalions of Swiss soldiers lodged, hidden and protected, in the crags of the Alps, while bridges and tunnels were set with dynamite, ready to be blown up to stop outside forces marching into the country. The Swiss ideal of neutrality did not mean a defenceless nation but instead had crystallised into an acute militaristic culture. A reversed Trojan Horse of sorts. But digital warfare changed the nature of the redoubt strategy: to counter data theft and cyberattacks on critical infrastructure, supercomputers and large data centres have joined traditional weapons and gold reserves underground.

Me weiss was cha passiere ("You know what can happen") is a phrase borrowed from a song of Swiss singer-songwriter Mani Matter (1936–1972). In the chanson "I Han Es Zündhölzli Azündt", Matter shows how small actions can have sweeping effects by describing how a matchstick drops on the carpet and consecutively sets the house, the town and ultimately the whole country on fire. In the lyrics, he reflects on the Swiss psyche by playing with the tensions between freedom, safety and a paranoid desire for control.

Swiss
Data
Safe

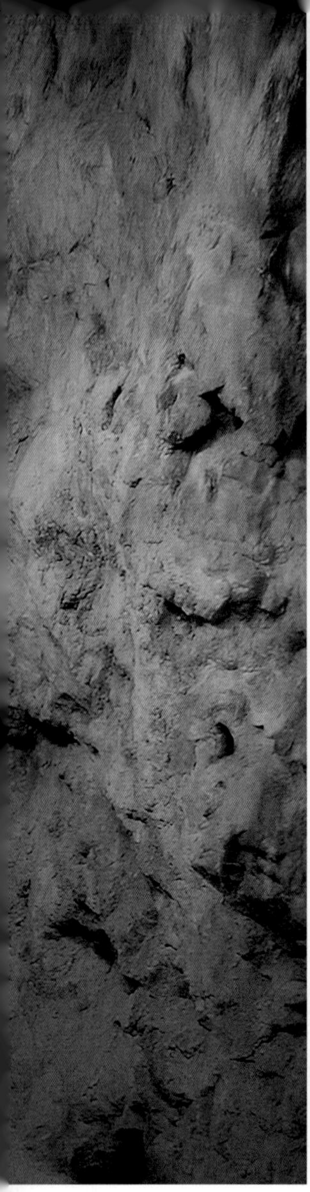

08

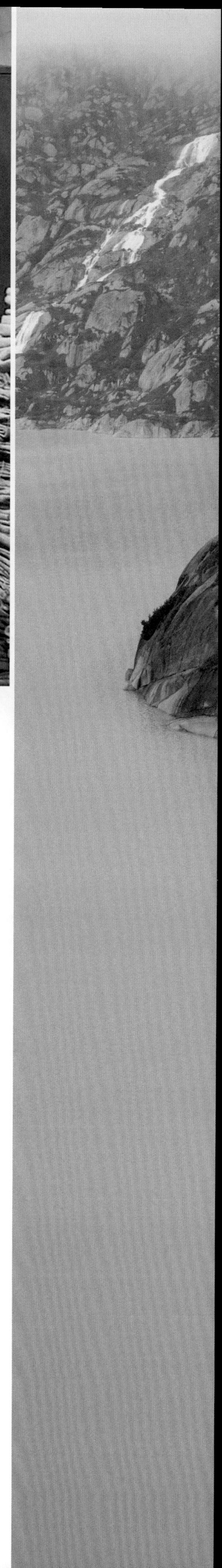

Wir investieren in erneuerbare Energien.
KWO
WOLFF

01

02

03

04

05

06

07

08

01 A glaciologist performs measurements at the glacier Grubengletscher, 1970. The boxes in front of him contain explosives that help carrying out seismic surveys. Accurate data and scientific knowledge about the Swiss alpine landscape was and still is of outmost importance for the country. It allowed for the planning, construction and maintenance of the Réduit system during World War II and after.

02 The Teufelsbrücke ("devils bridge") is traversing the Schöllen canyon, a strategically important site on the way to the Gotthard region in the centre of Switzerland. As many other roads, tunnels and bridges, the site was supposedly equipped with explosives, ready to be blown up in case a foreign army would invade the country.

03 Shooting slit for a camouflaged bunker canon at fortress Furggels. The combined range of all artillery weapons of the Swiss Réduit system was supposed to form a continuous line of fire throughout the central part of Switzerland.

04 A turret camouflaged as a stone, fortress Foppa Grande. The firing range of the fortress was 18–22 kilometres.

05 A turret camouflaged as a stone, fortress San Carlo. Situated at the Gotthard Pass, the fortress is situated at a crucial location and lies 2,060 metres above sea level.

06 A turret camouflaged as an alpine hut, fortress Furggels. The fortress hosted more than 400 members of the armed forces.

07 One of three turrets of fortress Magletsch, camouflaged as an alpine hut. The fortress is located underground, could host 381 soldiers and was protected by anti-aircraft guns against aerial attacks.

08 Two miners working on the construction of a fortress, using explosives and a jackhammer. The illustration is part of a postcard series from the Swiss military that propagated information about the construction of the Réduit system in 1939/40. Underneath the illustration, the postcard features the title "Somewhere in Switzerland" in order to keep the location of the bunker secret.

09

10

11

12

13

14

15

16

09 Shooting slits of fortress Tschingels. Carved out of the rock, the slits are located on the second of four floors. Built in 1940, the fortress was one of the biggest defensive structures in the East of Switzerland, designed for 160 soldiers, with the highest shooting slits 150 metres above the ground.

10 Specimen of a graphite-bearing slate from the Gotthard massif. The stone is part of a rock collection of the Swiss Federal Institute of Technology ETH, which was compiled during the construction of the Gotthard tunnel in the 1880s. Scientific collections and classifications like this helped to gather knowledge about the composition of Swiss mountains and subsequently control, extract and engineer the alpine territory for political and military purposes.

11 Soldiers operating a cannon in the fortress San Carlo. To operate the heavy weapon, 11 soldiers were needed.

12 Camouflaged entrance of the observation post of fortress Ebersberg.

13 Construction works on a bunker. The motive is part of a postcard series from the Swiss military from 1939/40. The illustrations were drawn by Swiss graphic artist Eric de Coulon (1888–1956), who created iconic tourism and advertisement posters for Switzerland too.

14 Entrance to the Bundesratsbunker K8, Amsteg. The bunker was built between 1940 and 1942 and was meant to protect the Swiss government in case of an invasion. Supposedly, one room in K8 was used for the storage of gold by the Swiss Federal bank until 1995.

15 Today, the decommissioned governmental bunker K8 hosts server farms, as well as high security storages for art, documents, precious metals and gems. The site is operated by the company Swiss Data Safe AG, whose owner, Dolf Wipfli, bought the former army complex in 1999. The company promotes itself as a place of “maximum security, discretion and service” to its customers, designed to survive a full-scale military attack. Furthermore, the safety structures of the bunker, with its ventilation, water supply and autonomous power plant, suit the operation of a datacentre, which needs constant cooling and a back-up power supply.

16 Servers of the datacentre Stollen Luzern. The operating company converted the former civil defense bunker and its tunnel system into a data storage space. It promotes itself as “green” because it uses hydropower and cold water from Lake Lucerne close by to cool down its servers.

17

18

19

20

21

22

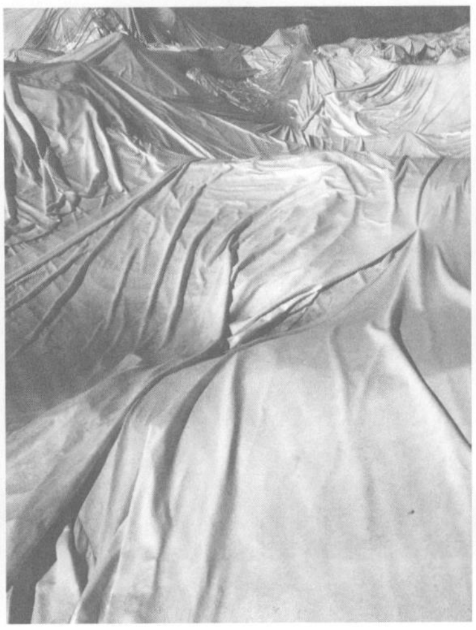

23

17 A signaling device in an underground research facility. The unregular wall structures block electromagnetic signals from the outside. This characteristic makes many Swiss bunkers attractive for high security datacentres.

18 Army personnel in front of Swiss military servers. The Swiss army has opened two new datacentres in its alpine territory in 2020 and wants to open another one until 2028. The sites occur costs of 3,8 billion Francs and are partly classified. The datacentres should serve as information hubs and digital command centres for military coordination.

19 Cables and pipes inside the Grimsel rock laboratory. Established during the cold war in 1984, the laboratory is located 450 metres beneath the surface. Its tunnels are one kilometre long and host research stations and data measuring systems that help investigating the suitability of rock formations for the long-term storage of nuclear waste.

20 Underground infrastructure of the former military fortress Furggels. Today, the bunker is owned by private investor Erich Breitenmoser who rents out spaces for cryptocurrency mining, data storage and scientific experiments. Fortress Furggels consists of 195 rooms, eight kilometres of tunnels, an emergency power generator and its own water reservoir.

21 Lake Grimsel is an artificial lake and a hydroelectric reservoir that helps to produce electricity by locking and unlocking the 114 metres high Spitallamm dam. Many Swiss datacentres are powered by hydroelectric energy and cooled down by lake water.

22 Parts of the Rhone glacier are covered with a tarpulin to slow down the melting process, driven by increased temperatures. Due to climate change, many Swiss glaciers are expected to vanish by 2090, which threatens the country's power supply that relies to more than 50 per cent on hydroelectric power. However, in the short term their melting water will create hundreds of new lakes and lead to greater electricity generation, which will make the implementation of datacentres in the Swiss alps more attractive.

23 The massive wall of the Spitallamm dam is replaced after 90 years of operation and an evolving crack. The new wall will consist of 220,000 cubic metres concrete. In order to make use of the increased meltwater flows from glaciers, Switzerland plans to renovate existing dams, but also to carve new water tunnels into mountains, install more generating plants and build new dams.

KATRIN S

NIGHT TI

102

TREICHER

E TREMOR

103

S

104

ANXIETY COLLAPSE COMMODIFIED NATURE EROSION EXTRACTION PERSECUTION OF INDIGENOUS COMMUNITIES RECLAMATION RETROFITTING SUBSIDENCE SWEDEN TIRED BODIES

There are cracks in the walls of Kiruna's homes. The centre of the northernmost town in Sweden is threatened by the Kiirunavaara mine, which is also the reason for its existence. At the beginning of the 20th century, the Luossavaara-Kiirunavaara Aktiebolag, a state-owned mining company, broke grounds to exploit the ore buried deep in the Earth of Lapland, the territory of the Sami people. The only year-long mechanical connection to the rest of the country was a train line dedicated to the transport of the precious sediment. Exploited continuously since 1900, the mine was soon surrounded by a town that has been home to up to 25,000 souls. But subsidence, the mining-related collapse of the Earth's surface, now threatens the city's town centre with fissures in the hospital and a school that needed to be abandoned. The night-time tremors of underground explosions tear off the ore from the mountain, shake the bowels of the Earth and weaken the wall of the constructions above. The city will move, building after building, deconstructed and reconstructed, or lifted and placed on lorries. Three kilometres east, a new/old Kiruna has started taking shape. Within a couple of decades, the old town centre will be abandoned, and will eventually be swallowed by the relentless consumption of the Kiruna landscape.

Berlin-based photographer Katrin Streicher has carried out several trips to Kiruna to photograph the quotidian of its inhabitants, the slow change of a landscape that makes people's wealth as well as their predicament. The people, the mining industry, the landscape, are intertwined characters whose hopes and anxiety, strength and fracture, answer each other in the dead of night.

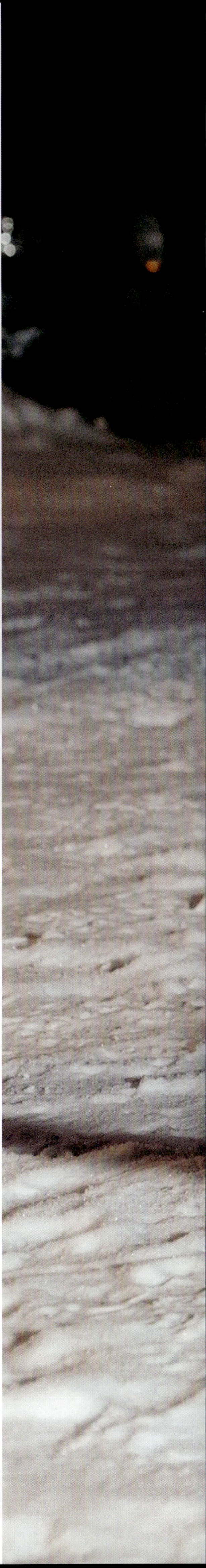

BIANCO®
FOOTWEAR

CRAFT
CRAFT
KIRUNA KOMMUN
Miljökontoret

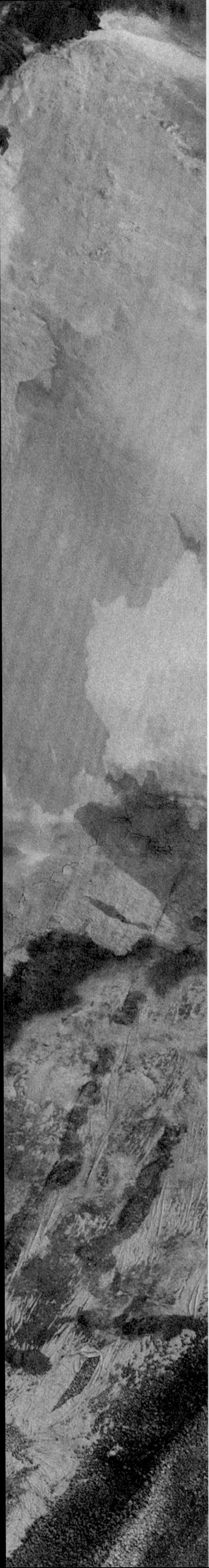

01

02

03

04

05

06

07

08

01 The city of Kiruna changes its face. The old town hall, a landmark of the city, has already been torn town. The roof above the entrance gate was left behind to memorise the building.
02 The Ullspiran housing complex is located very close to the mine and the buildings will be among the first homes to be torn down.
03 Teenagers from Kiruna spend one of the long polar nights in their EPA tractor on a parking lot close to Luossavaara mountain; the sky is painted orange from the lights of Kiruna's huge iron ore mine.
04 Explosives underground in Kirunavaara mountain are used to extract iron. The blasts that happen every night at 2 am cause the earth to tremor. The shaking earth can be felt throughout Kiruna.
05 Mining in Kiruna leads to seismic activities and tremors occurring in the bedrock. Geophones are placed all over Kiruna to monitor these activities.
06 Maija plays outside with her dog in the polar night.
07 Kiruna Town Hall is one of the first buildings to be moved from its current location to the new city centre.
08 Stone wall along one of the approximately 500 kilometre long roads that wind through LKAB's iron ore mine in mount Kiirunavaara. The roads go underground to a depth of 1365 metres.

09

10

11

12

13

14

15

16

09 Åke photograped in his home in the Ullspiran area in Kiruna. The houses of Ullspiran are very close to the mine and are the first buildings to be torn down, because they are no longer safe for living. He and his family have in the meantime relocated to a new house.
10 One of Kiruna's residential streets at night.
11 Stone wall along one of the approximately 500 kilometre long roads that wind through LKAB's iron ore mine in mount Kiirunavaara. The roads go underground to a depth of 1365 m.
12 Cafeteria 540 metres under ground in Kiruna's iron ore mine.
13 Around Kirunavaara mine lies a huge area of land coined by the mining process. Mining by-products like Bentonit are deposited here.
14 Kiruna's iron ore mine at night.
15 Tuollavaara iron ore mine was closed down in 1980. The two towers were kept as a landmark. The new city centre of Kiruna is being built right next to the old mine.
16 A drilling machine 540 metres underground in Kiruna's iron ore mine.

CHARLOTTE MALTERRE-BARTHES

ARCHITECTURE OF EXTRACTION

A tentative political economy of space and the built environment

[Human]'s ability to participate intelligently in the evolution of [its] own system is dependent on [its] ability to perceive the whole.
Immanuel Wallerstein, *The Modern World-System* (2011)

The Anthropocene as a politically infused geology and scientific/popular discourse is just now noticing the extinction it has chosen to continually overlook in the making of its modernity and freedom.
Kathryn Yusoff, *A Billion Black Anthropocenes or None* (2018)

Concrete, steel, glass, brick, wood, and a myriad of oil-based products are the materials most prevalently used in construction worldwide. Made of crushed stone, gravel, limestone, clay, iron ore, aluminium diatomite, kaolin, bentonite, silica, barite, gypsum, potash, pumice, talc, petroleum, these processed minerals make up our built environment. Facilitation technologies that allow for the building industry to function through connected objects (i.e. software, hardware, phones, data centres, measuring devices, information networks, GPS-led engines) also require processed minerals and rare earths (i.e. barium, chromite, coltan, copper, dolomite, feldspar, gallium, germanium, gold, halite, indium, lead, lithium, manganese, mercury, mica, nickel, quartz, silicon, silver, sulphite, tantalum, tin, tungsten, uranium, and zinc). These minerals are extracted via socially, ecologically, and physically destructive techniques. Furthermore, the so-called "ecological transition" and its attending policies are expected to stimulate and increase demand for "green infrastructure." These so-called "clean" and "green" technologies – such as solar-powered heating, and e-cars – rely on more resource mining, not less.[1] Deeply entrenched in these procedures of matter transformation, the construction industry's devastating nature is well-known, its CO_2 output quantified. However, the way that these aspects relate to its political economy is ignored as the status quo prevails. Debt economy, speculative financing, neo-colonial export politics and labour conditions, racist mining, and exploitative design/construction practices are some of the many nefarious arrangements that shape the architecture of our lives, a reality that actors along the supply chain of space production, from banks to design offices, continue to disregard. To redress this myopia, there is a need for a tentative outline of a political economy of space and of the built environment.

SKETCHING A POLITICAL ECONOMY OF THE BUILT ENVIRONMENT

Engaging with an analysis of how a sum of commodities is turned into another commodity, space, is an attempt to refuse the detachment of design disciplines regarding the damage done by the construction industry, from mining to real estate, and from investment to a building site, as part of the Anthropocene. To alter the way we think about the attending systems that fuel body exhaustion, social devastation, land sealing, carbon emissions, and global resource depletion to generate capital accumulation is an essential stepping stone toward identifying leverage points for an insurgent design practice. Scholars attempted the arduous task of untangling material histories and exploitation, from Mimi Sheller's *Aluminium Dreams* (2014) to Kenneth Warren's *Big Steel* (2008), or with Thea Riofranco's research on lithium *Resource Radicals* (2020). If in those works, the link to the built environment is at time tenuous, it is addressed frontally by

1 Jillian Ambrose, 'Green Economy Plans Fuel New Metals and Energy 'Supercycle',' *The Guardian* (2021). https://www.theguardian.com/business/2021/jan/10/green-economy-plans-fuel-new-metals-and-energy-supercycle.

Matthew Gandy's *Concrete and Clay* (2002) on the manipulation of nature in the making of New York City, or by Kiel Moe's research on the environmental weight of buildings *Empire, State & Building* (2017). Jane Mah Hutton both in *Reciprocal Landscapes* (2020), and with the edited volume *Material Culture* (2018) wonderfully unravels a history of material flows uncovering exploitative realities behind the violent ways of making the built environment. The historical role of commodities in shaping spaces is also at the heart of the seminal *Nature's Metropolis* by William Cronon (1991), which traces the link between the city and its productive hinterlands, drawing grain, timber and meat.[2]

Explicating the rise of capitalism through the wrenching global impact of cotton produced by slave labor, Sven Beckert's *Empire of Cotton* (2014) is a compelling articulation of the consumption of everything, grounded in Emanuel Wallerstein's world systems theory.[3] This research path is also the one Raj Patel and Jason Moore followed and expanded with *A History of the World in Seven Cheap Things* (2017), on the role of material production and violent extraction in the discounting of nature.[4]

Carola Hein's *Oil Spaces* (2022) tackles the understudied role of fossil fuel in the production of the modern world, with a contemporary onlook close to Timothy Mitchell's *Carbon Democracy* (2011). Research on sand, soil, and extractive practices has also produced excellent scholarship, notably with Alexandra Arènes's work on Earth's critical zone or Michael Welland's investigation on the sand.[5] Mineral extraction, territory, and labour are brilliantly examined by Martín Arboleda in *Planetary Mine* (2020), and by Mazen Labban with "Deterritorializing Extraction: Bioaccumulation and the Planetary Mine," as well as by Sergio Ferro in "Concrete as Weapon."[6] Uncovering the relationships between materials, labour, and race, Kathryn Yusoff's seminal work on white geology, slavery, and mining, *A Billion Black Anthropocenes or None* (2018), intersects with environmental racism research among others, as does Imani Jacqueline Brown's research with Forensic Architecture on "Death Alley" in Louisiana, and Katherine McKittricks' enormously influential geographic exploration of black bodies in *Demonic Grounds*.[7] Among the pieces mentioned in this brief review, not all have an approach grounded in political economy. Surprisingly, despite neoliberalism being a well-studied topic with numerous scholarly efforts to study its emergence and expansion, the spatialization of commodified materials is not well studied within design disciplines. Thus the present

2 See William Cronon, *Nature's Metropolis: Chicago and the Great West* (New York: W.W. Norton, 1991).

3 See Sven Beckert, *Empire of Cotton: A Global History* (New York: Alfred A. Knopf, 2014).

4 See Raj Patel and Jason W. Moore, *A History of the World in Seven Cheap Things: A Guide to Capitalism, Nature, and the Future of the Planet* (Oakland, California: University of California Press, 2017).

5 Alexandra Arènes, Bruno Latour, and Jérôme Gaillardet, 'Giving Depth to the Surface: An Exercise in the Gaia-Graphy of Critical Zones', *The anthropocene review* 5, no. 2 (2018); Michael Welland, *Sand: The Never-Ending Story* (Berkeley: University of California Press, 2009).

6 Mazen Labban, 'Deterritorializing Extraction: Bioaccumulation and the Planetary Mine,' *Annals of the Association of American Geographers* 104, no. 3 (2014); Sérgio Ferro, 'Concrete as Weapon', *Harvard Design Magazine*, no. 46 (2018).

effort seeks to articulate an interconnected view of the political economy of space, aiming at a critique of the contemporary forms of resource extraction, labour exhaustion, land appropriation, and commodified construction enabled by exploitative economies. To critically examine space production logics, actors, and locales, from global capital to the home, from real estate investment to concrete production, we must shift our perception of the built environment from an innocent set of separated forces, responsibilities, and actors to conceive of an intentionally enacted supply chain of space production, singular yet multiple.

THE SUPPLY CHAIN OF SPACE PRODUCTION

As a means of production, commodified space and its "component elements (nature, labour, technology, knowledge); structures (property relations); superstructures (institutions and the state itself)" are key to the capitalist economy.[8] However, the space production supply chain is rarely understood and is yet to be fully delineated. To consider the entire production chain from the field to the home requires looking closely at agents, actions, and materiality: How is space produced, and what is it made of? Who is labouring for it, and at what costs? What are the locales engaged? Many forces, actors, and transactions, from funding and legislating to designing and organising, propel the extraction, transportation, processing, and installation of construction materials, allocating, exploiting, inhabiting, and finally demolishing and discarding. To disentangle some of the complexity inherent to the dynamics of all commodity chains, the present method reflects the examination narrated by Karl Marx in *A Contribution to the Critique of the Political Economy* (1859, English translation 1904), in which the economic system is approached through capital, land, labour, state, foreign trade, and world markets. In *The Condition of Postmodernity* (1990), the Marxist geographer David Harvey underlines the pertinence of such a method: "Marx begins *Capital*, […], with an analysis of commodities […]. Yet the commodity IS, he avers, 'a mysterious thing' because it simultaneously embodies both a use value (it fulfils a particular want or need) and an exchange value (I can use it as a bargaining chip to procure other commodities)."[9] This particular focus on commodity allows us to articulate a holistic view of the supply chain of space production. It entails identifying all these sectors, stages, and agents in their political-economic agencies and the elements, forces, and moments in the chain that drives extraction, construction, and urbanisation.

Reinscribing space production as a commodity and a linear flow allows for refuting the separation between land, property, labour, matter, and design.

7 Nina Wexelblatt and others, 'Round Table: Landscapes and Logics of Extractivism,' *Thresholds* (Cambridge, Mass.), no. 49 (2021); Katherine McKittrick, *Demonic Grounds: Black Women and the Cartographies of Struggle* (Minneapolis: University of Minnesota Press, 2006).

8 Henri Lefèbvre, *The Production of Space (La Production De L'espace,* Oxford: Blackwell, 1991/1974).

9 David Harvey, *The Condition of Postmodernity: An Enquiry into the Origins of Cultural Change* (Oxford: Blackwell, 1990), 100.

The concept of commodity chains as "a network of labour and production processes whose end result is a finished commodity" holds potential for illuminating actors and forces involved in commodity flows and contributing an approach to the political economy of space.[10] A more advanced form of investigation derived from world-systems theory is the *commodity chain analysis* defined as "composed of a series of operations or transformations, a set of agents and a system of markets (in terms of both physical flows and their monetary equivalents), as well as the behaviour of the agents as guided by their economic interests."[11] Agents involved in space production include those who contribute directly and act upon the transformation of land into a built commodity through markets: financing agents, public entities, real estate developers, designers and engineers, contractors, construction laborers, users, and maintenance agents, as well as players with indirect yet significant inputs: mining companies, transportation agents, processing agents, traders, and material suppliers. Among those agents, some perform multiple roles (e.g. financing agents-real estate developers, contractors-owners). Following a commodity chain analysis is consistent with articulating this supply chain from the cradle to the grave. The last segments encompass demolition and waste management agents and redevelopment and gentrification forces – as the endless cycle of recapitalisation engulfs space production. Identifying these actors uncovers a political economy of space where over-accumulation and fictitious capital play a central role. To each actor corresponds an action: financing, land banking and acquisition, building design, legal approval, material sourcing, construction, operating, sale, renovation, demolition, and site redevelopment, as well as resource extracting, transportation, processing, and distribution. It summarises the concatenation of these actors and the material actions that composes the space production supply chain.

There is obscurity as to who drives the financialisation of space and the differentiated role of influential private and public entities. If the origins of every built project lay within the intensification of capital-driven urbanisation processes spanning across all scales from the molecular to the planetary, the financialisation segment is undoubtedly one of the most opaque in this supply chain.[12] David Harvey, Manuel Castells, Saskia Sassen, and Neil Brenner, to name but a few, studied extensively "spaces of capital," producing precious critical geographies and uncovering mechanisms behind the commodification of land.[13] Against the backdrop of global capital, financial and governance agents, economic ideologies, and instruments shape the contours of the current po-

10 Philip Raikes, Michael Friis Jensen, and Stefano Ponte, 'Global Commodity Chain Analysis and the French Filière Approach: Comparison and Critique,' *Economy and Society* 29, no. 3 (2000), 409.

11 Fabien Tallec and Louis Bockel, 'Commodity Chain Analysis: Constructing the Commodity Chain Functional Analysis and Flow Charts,' *Rome: UN Food and Agriculture Organization*, (2005), 2.

12 Neil Brenner, 'What Is Critical Urban Theory?,' *City* 13, no. 2–3 (2009).

litical economy of space. Because land is a finite commodity, it is not merely investors, banks, hedge funds, and global real estate firms that fuel space production as a value-generating process. The entire global financial stock – including bank deposits, government and private debt securities, and equities also seeks to generate value through construction. Furthermore, the entanglements between private and public capital among the global finance actors post-2008 signify the delineation between state and investors is imprecise. For instance, precedents across the board have shown that state intervention in real estate matters takes various forms: privatisation of social housing to create mortgage borrowing, state-owned infrastructure and land sold at discounted prices to investors, or "accumulation by dispossession" with land acquired via public expropriation resold to developers.[14] Such intricacies parse the process of space production with a myriad of actors converging towards the act of construction.

In the western world, a project's stimulus is usually with private investors or clients or propelled by public entities with a capital or access to banking loans that commission via a series of various protocols and service providers (transactional, management, valuing, reporting, insurance agents), a design or engineering office to develop a site. Land acquisition is essential to this process. Public actors (government agencies, municipalities, ministries, universities, etc.) may already own land or have the legal tools to acquire plots by dispossession or facilitating property transfer to the private sector. For the private sector, entities might commission traders or find land to purchase – either unbuilt ("green," "raw") or previously built ("brown"). If necessary, a planning or design office is commissioned to develop a master plan or a subdivision complying with zoning and regulations, which is then sanctioned by public entities, at times undergoing public hearings protocols. Once validated, the installation of public infrastructures (road, water, facilities, etc.) and the conduction of safety surveys (seismic, environmental, etc.) are undertaken by the government or commissioned with a contractor. If the project envisioned is large or complex, a design agency is contracted by the investor/developer to design further the project, as well as to consult with structural engineers, hire contractors, manage, and follow the construction process to its completion and delivery. Depending on local regulations, home builders might undertake the construction of their single-family houses themselves. Building elements are sourced to erect the building based on availability, commodity costs, and design choices. Secondary agents come into play as contractors (smaller firms and labourers, i.e. plumbers and electricians) and order the construction materials. While these are often readily available, their production is nestled in the supply chain of extracted goods.

13 See David Harvey, *The Urbanization of Capital* (Oxford: Blackwell, 1985); Saskia Sassen, *The Global City: New York, London, Tokyo* (Princeton: Princeton University Press, 1991); Manuel Castells, *The Urban Question: A Marxist Approach* (Cambridge: MIT Press, 1979); Neil Brenner and Nikolas Theodore, *Spaces of Neoliberalism : Urban Restructuring in North America and Western Europe* (Oxford: Blackwell, 2002).

14 Richard Waldron, 'Capitalizing on the State: The Political Economy of Real Estate Investment Trusts and the 'Resolution' of the Crisis,' *Geoforum* 90, (2018).

Various trading agents (e.g., local and cooperative traders, brokers, public agencies, trading houses) buy and sell construction commodities even before processing. A host of actors are mobilised for minerals extraction, processing and manufacturing, and transportation to the building site, activities that engage labour, machinery, fuel consumption, infrastructures, and industrial processes. Since each construction commodity, from concrete foundations to balloon-frame wood structures, to electric outlets and insulation roofing polymers, requires a specific and distinct set of actors, the ramifications of the industry are gigantic, its impact massive. In addition, there are all the agents driving the "productive technology of large-scale industry" that facilitate all operations along the supply chain of space production, from trading terminals to design tasks, and these too must be accounted for.[15] Once the building is completed, large investors (pension and hedge funds, insurance forms, real-estate trusts) lease and manage the property or sell the units. Users (renters, owners) occupy and maintain the space. Often ignored and devalued, maintenance and reparation agents are invisible but important actors that upkeep and prolong buildings' lives. Finally, at the end of the chain, demolition and recycling agents undertake the task of dismantling structures and disposing of materials and waste.

While grounded in Marxist philosophy, this holistic view of the supply chain of space given by identifying all stages and agents is insufficient if it only remains a descriptive reading. Another step is necessary: to connect every move of the spatialised power dynamics of capital accumulation to social and racial injustice, colonial and neo-colonial schemes, and extractive processes. In other words, understanding all actions and actors along the commodity chain of space production forms the first stage of a broader uncovering of the role of commodified construction, refuting the ongoing human and ecological devastation. Identifying the mechanisms of space production and organisation is a necessary study that articulates a mandate for design disciplines to act upon the elements, forces, and moments along the chain. By doing so, several canonical and scientific legitimacies are suspended. What is objected to here is the notion that the forces that bear impacts on architecture, urban forms, and territory are beyond the purview of design disciplines.

Moreover, what is also refused is the view that designers have no leverage on the space production commodity chain and thus no part in the injustice and damage it generates. This is not as much disempowering as it is untrue, as it ignores the "shadow geology of disposable lives, waste, toxicity, contamination, extinction, and exhaustion" design and construction fuel.[16] Only with a total acknowledgment and full understating of this role can there be a conceivable future for space production practices.

15 Martin Arboleda, *Planetary Mine: Territories of Extraction under Late Capitalism* (London/New York: Verso, 2020), 41.

16 Kathryn Yusoff, *A Billion Black Anthropocenes or None* (Minneapolis, MN : University Of Minnesota Press, 2018), 34.

ELINE BE

ELIAS KI

FOOTPRIN

138

JAMINSE

AIYO

S IN THE

139

VALLEY

[DE/NEO/POST]COLONIALISM AFRICAPITALISM COMMODIFIED NATURE DEATH FORESTS GREENHOUSE GAS HEGEMONY KENYA PERIPHERIES PERSECUTION OF INDIGENOUS COMMUNITIES REGULATIONS TECHNOSOLUTIONISM TREES AS INFRASTRUCTURE

What happens when you tick the box that certifies the journey of your air-travelled international parcel will be "carbon-free"? Or when you are guilt-tripped to pay the three euros to "plant a tree" when booking a plane ticket for your holidays? Visual artist Eline Benjaminsen asked herself that very question and started an ongoing journey to visit *her* tree, planted somewhere in a Kenyan forest. In "Footprints in the Valley", Benjaminsen opens a new episode of her densely layered, multimedia investigations that focus on the localised expressions of international infrastructure and their network.

In her previous project, "Where the money is made", she had explored through photographic "follow-the-money" narratives, as she calls them, the tangible manifestations of market processes across space and time. In "Footprints in the valley", Benjaminsen takes apart carbon offsetting, the virtual reduction or removal of one's carbon emissions by the implementation of carbon negative designs elsewhere—typically the planting of a tree that is meant to capture CO_2 emissions.

In her project, which involves close collaboration with activist and Sengwer indigenous community leader Elias Kimaiyo, who has contributed a text on the Sengwer defence of their land in addition to Benjaminsen's series in this book, Benjaminsen questions the neo-colonial stammering that sees corporations and governments of the Global North, pouring money in countries of the Global South in the name of sustainability, with no comprehension, nor any careful appraisal of the repercussions for indigenous communities on the ground. Her project raises important questions on our instrumentalisation of "nature", its commodification in the name of sustainability, the virtual transfer of Global North countries' pollution to others' land, and the fantasy of carbon offsetting—or the mirage that privileged Global North societies can continue polluting, for there will always be remote lands, implicitly understood as less-developed and inferior, to bear the burden of their waste.

FEVERPITCH
WILL UNITED
STOP SPURS?

POLITICS: Raila attacks Uhuru over resource sharing, PAGE 9
THE STANDARD
Kenya's Bold Newspaper
Thursday, December 1, 2016
KCSE COPY-PASTE EDITION
Mathematics questions lifted from past papers
CORRUPTION WAR
Kalonzo Musyoka
Alfred Mutua
Patrick Makau
Sh30M
4,000

01

02

03

04

05

06

07

08

01 Remains of a torched Sengwer house, Kapkok glade.
02 Detail: rendering of Rosewood, Embobut. Estimated above-ground carbon stock: 2.4 tons.
03 Elias Kimaiyo: "The Kenyan Forest Service has often burned our houses and denied it. As evidence, I photograph the burning houses with the day's newspaper in front of them."
04 Water collection. Still from video: Treewounds, 2021.
05 Digital rendering of Cedar, Embobut. Circumference: 426 centimetres. Height: 40 metres. Estimated above-ground carbon stock: 8.74 tons. Digital rendering.
06 Detail: rendering of Stotwo, Embobut. Estimated above-ground carbon stock: 3.38 tons.
07 Beehive making. Still from video: Treewounds, 2021.
08 Remains of torched Sengwer house, Kapkok glade.
09 Detail: rendering of Stotwo, Embobut. Estimated above-ground carbon stock: 3.38 tons.
10 A burned house photographed by Kimaiyo with the day's newspaper as a timestamp.

09

10

11

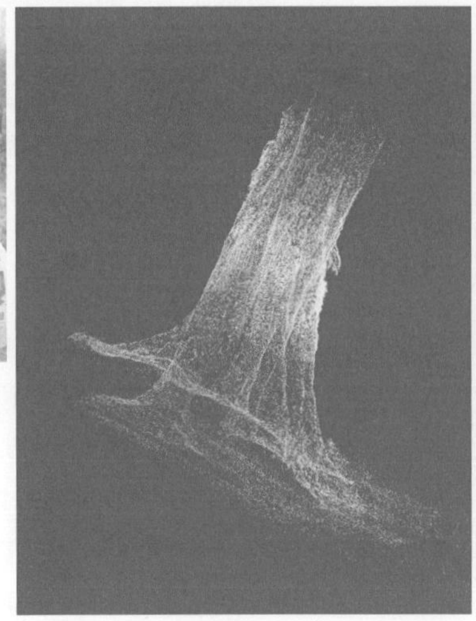

12

13

14

15

11 Rosewood, Embobut. Circumference: 256 centimetres. Height: 20 metres. Estimated above-ground carbon stock: 2.46 tons. Digital rendering.
12 Detail: rendering of Stotwo, Embobut. Estimated above-ground carbon stock: 3.38 tons.
13 Elias Kimayio: "Sheep grazing in Kapkok glade at a place called Marichor in Embobut. Sengwer are traditionally hunter-gatherers but since the government banned hunting in the 1970s, herding has become one of our primary livelihood activities."
14 Sheep grazing in Marichor, Embobut.
15 Elias Kimayio: "A place called Kipsitona in Kapkok glade where a Sengwer man named Robert was murdered by guards from the Kenyan Forest Service who were carrying out evictions in January 2018. After shooting him, the guards dragged the body and hid it under this naturally fallen tree."

It is estimated that around a thousand Sengwer households have been torched by the Kenyan Forest Service (KFS) in the past decade. Arbitrary arrests of Sengwer community members have taken place despite an active court order issued by the court of appeal that restraints KFS from carrying out such acts. This has been done to intimidate us to leave the forest so that the area complies with conservation regulations that make it possible for the government to receive funds on the pretext of conservation. We have been called "squatters", "criminals" and recently "militia" to warrant these brutal and forceful evictions. But our livelihoods and culture are interwoven with the forest ecosystem. Our struggles with conservation politics date back to British colonial rule and are continued today through the funding arriving from the Global North, mainly the European Union and other European governments.

One of these so-called conservation projects relates to an ambition to calculate carbon stock: REDD+ (Reducing emissions through deforestation and forest degradation). An effort, in other words, to apply finance to the carbon stored in the ecosystems of our ancestral lands that we have been conserving since time immemorial. If this succeeds, it would be possible for governments elsewhere to boast they reduced their carbon emission, but on the contrary, by bankrolling "conservation" programmes in the Global South that commodify nature. This form of green capitalism results in the brutal displacing of the rightful owners and custodians of the targeted ecosystems.

After enduring many years of violations, 2022 has been one without forceful evictions. We are now rebuilding our lives, rebuilding our homes, restoring our livelihoods that were hampered by forceful evictions in the past. Finally, we are again able to keep bees, which is an essential Sengwer cultural activity that was made impossible for many years due to the KFS's harassment. Recently we trained community healthcare promoters and are continuing to train paralegals. We have also launched a training programme for community youth filmmakers who can help tell our story. In a direct, unmediated way, we can talk about our relation to forest lands. This will give agency to the community and provide us with a way to speak for ourselves, amplify our story and struggle for land rights.

Our advocacy against Western conservation theories has somewhat yielded positive results in stopping evictions because of the EU cancelling conservation funding that targeted our community land. It took the death of a Sengwer man, shot by Kenya Forest Service guards and another one seriously injured to stop the European programme. But a long-term solution is yet to be reached.

At the moment, we are engaging several stakeholders at both county and national levels to convince the government and its administration to adopt a human-based approach in all conservation projects, and more so take in on land tenure rights for Sengwer community where free, prior and informed consent is applied at all times.

My message to European citizens is that their taxes are used to displace us in the name of conservation projects, they should stop. In truth, such conservation funds cause great harm to indigenous people and their environment as it destroys communities and hurt their ways of life and culture. Not the least, is it hurtful to the nature that is supposedly conserved within these projects.

The problem of what we have been going through is because of these funds. If you want to send money to the Global South, you should come up with strong safeguard policies where indigenous peoples are involved in drafting the policies in order to mitigate against human rights violations. People in Europe need to understand that indigenous and local communities around the world are the best experts at conserving the forests they live in using their indigenous knowledge.

Last year, the president announced an effort to plant 15 billion trees in Kenya by 2032. As our struggle with past conservation schemes has taught us a thing or two, we decided to get ahead of the curve and have started to raise some seedlings of our own. We are raising indigenous tree seedlings and growing them in suitable areas of our land. If this was left to the government, they could bring the wrong type of tree species and plant them in unsuitable areas. In the worst case, this could turn out to be an invasive species, causing more harm to our ecosystem than good. In this way, we can keep custodianship of our forests, and still allow the government to reach their tree-planting goals.

The peace we are currently experiencing is happening because foreign donors to the conservation programme have backed down. This means the government has started to listen to us more, no longer only to the money. A good move towards the future.

Elias Kimaiyo is a Sengwer indigenous community leader from Embobut forest. He is also an environment, human and land rights defender as well as a community journalist. Together with other community leaders he lobbies for ancestral land tenure rights and recognition as a distinct tribe in Kenya. Kimaiyo works closely with community allies like civil societies, journalists, researchers and paralegals.

SALVATOR

DEATH BY

164

E VITALE

GPS

165

"Death by GPS" examines how biases in automation impact relationships between individuals, labour and social structures resulting in new forms of exploitation. The first part of the work draws parallels with the historical struggles of the working class against machines, focusing on the region of Gauteng, South Africa, and the connection between the gig economy, mining industry and technological sabotage. Salvatore Vitale's project spans from the depths of South African gold mines to the rooms of freelancers, where the technological age is unfolding. Through small acts of technological sabotage, "Death by GPS" prompts reflection on why the future is not working.

The project takes on a transmedia narrative format that incorporates documentary, fiction, and generative storytelling and it involves the collaboration of various freelancers hired through online gig platforms to create content. Ultimately, Vitale's ongoing project is a mixtape that includes a video collage, essay film, photographs, and music video, infused with internet virality to offer a thought-provoking depiction of the impact of automation on the exploitation of labour in the gig economy.

Named after the circumlocution describing individuals who did not question their GPS indications and encountered an untimely death, this project traces exploitation in the digital world, with a subversive visual and conceptual turn including the destruction of machines that threaten the existing socio-economic structure of a community, protest movements and their repression as well as our blind trust in technology and their billionaire messiahs. Through a multi-layered approach, "Death by GPS" connects the technosocial imaginary of the Global North and its relationship to the concept of "progress", together with the extraction of natural resources—such as gold and platinum—in countries of the Global South, like South Africa, where Vitale locates most of his initial research.

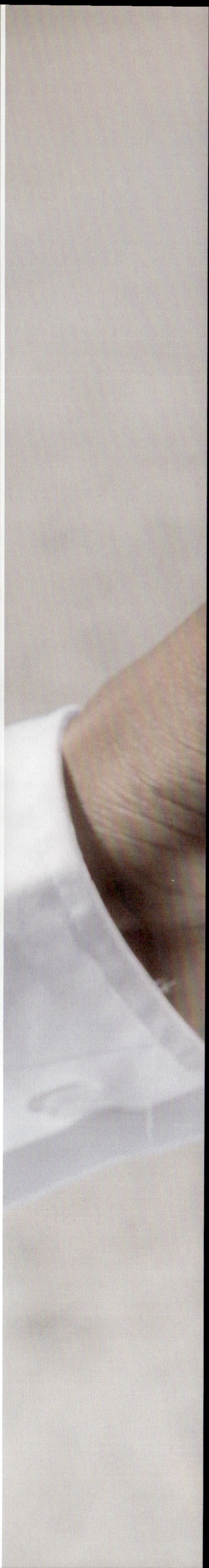

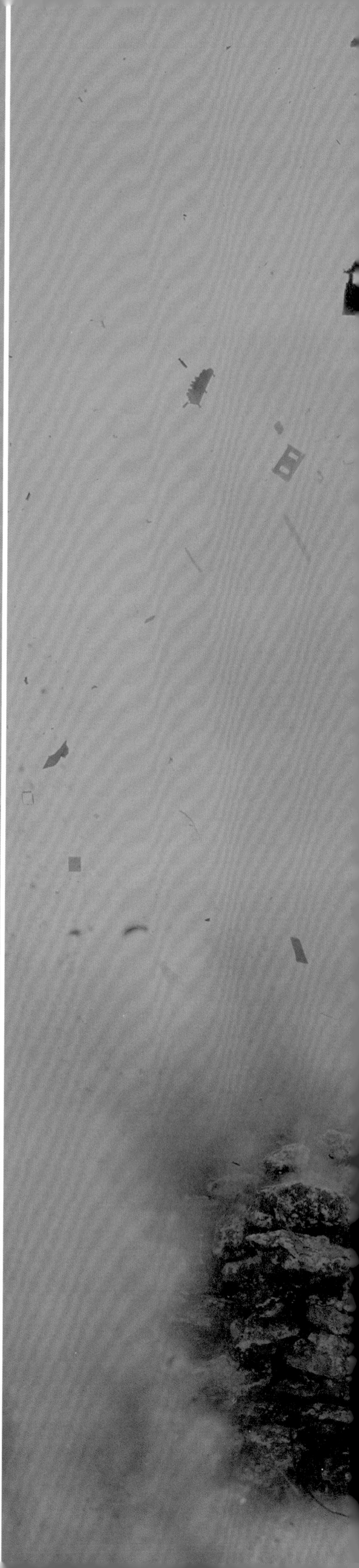

ECU

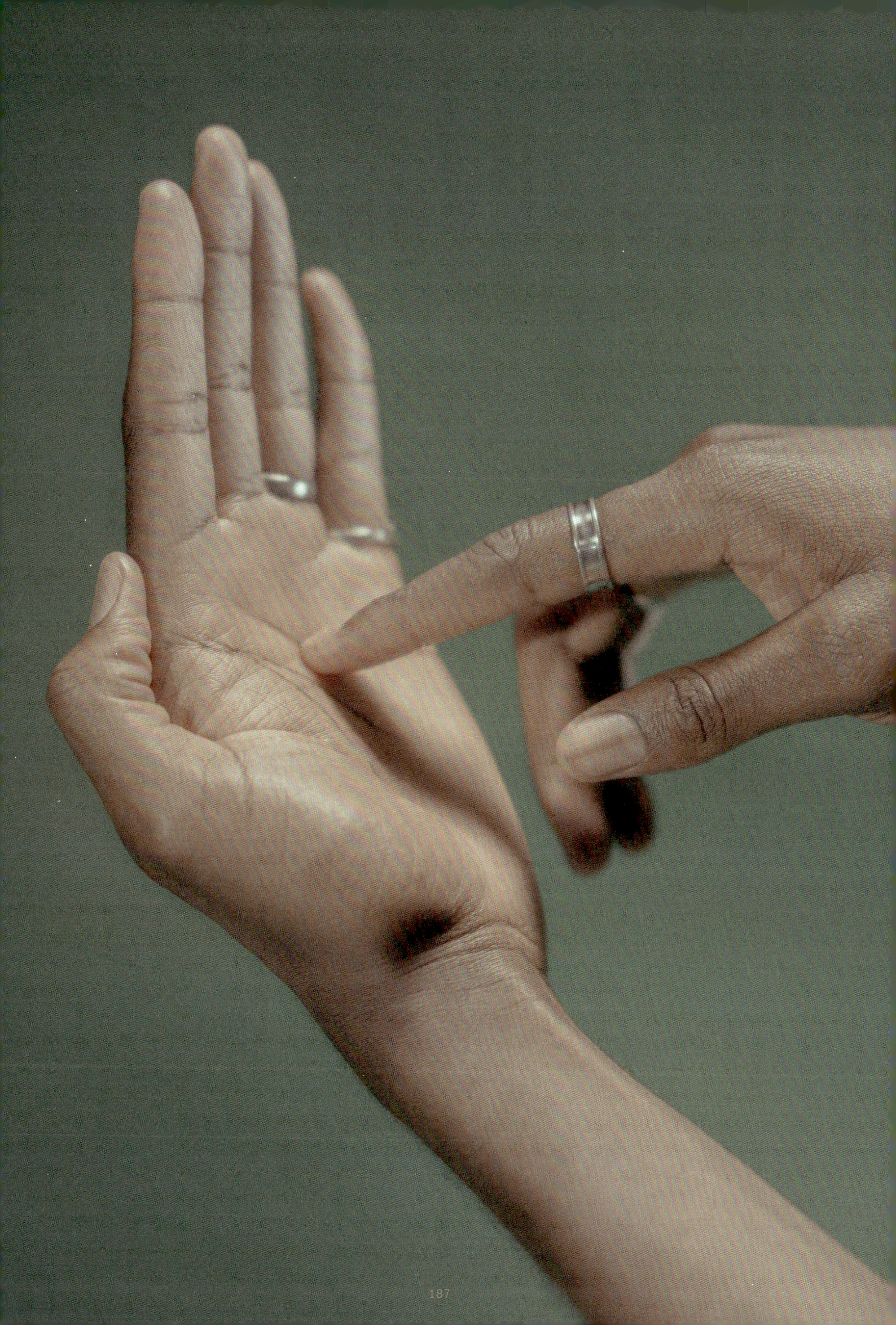

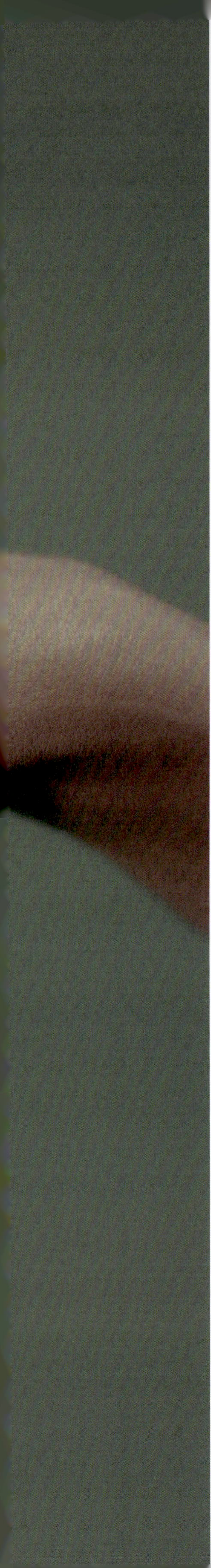

01

02

03

04

05

06

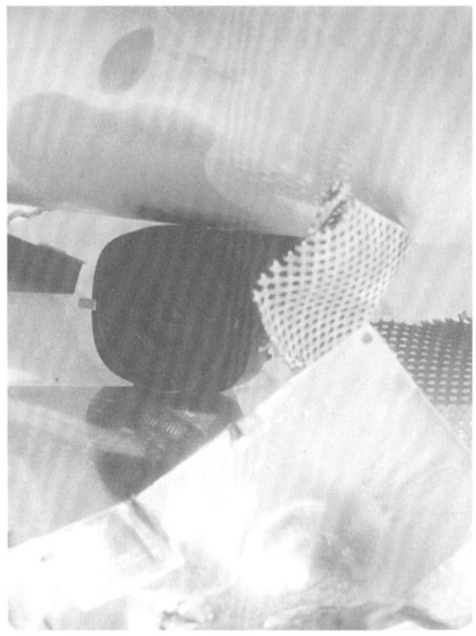

07

08

01 “We’re already cyborgs. Your phone and your computer are extensions of you, but the interface is through finger movements or speech, which are very slow.” from Death by GPS, 2022–ongoing.

02 “A company is a group organized to create a product or service, and it is only as good as its people and how excited they are about creating.” from “Death by GPS”, 2022–ongoing.

03 “An email saying you have gold is not the same as having gold.” from Death by GPS, 2022–ongoing

04 “We are excited for future!” from “Death by GPS”, 2022–ongoing.

05 “An email saying you have gold is not the same as having gold.” from Death by GPS, 2022–ongoing.

06 “It’s getting confusing out there. Let’s get organized. #2”, from Death by GPS, 2022–ongoing.

09.A

09.B

09.C

10.A

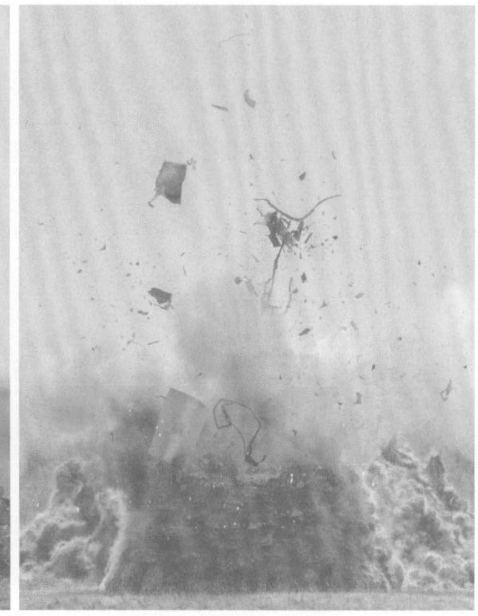

10.B

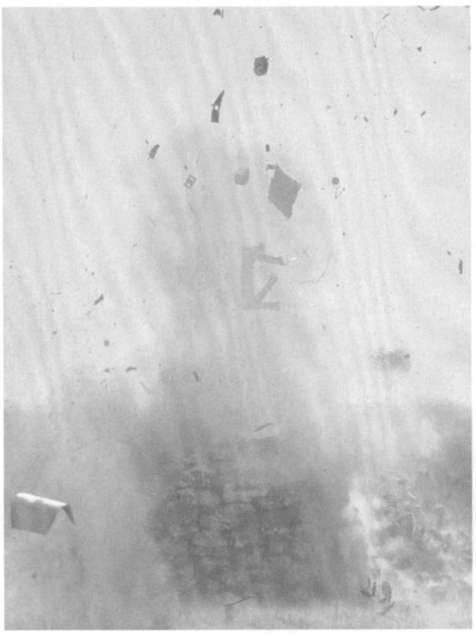

10.C

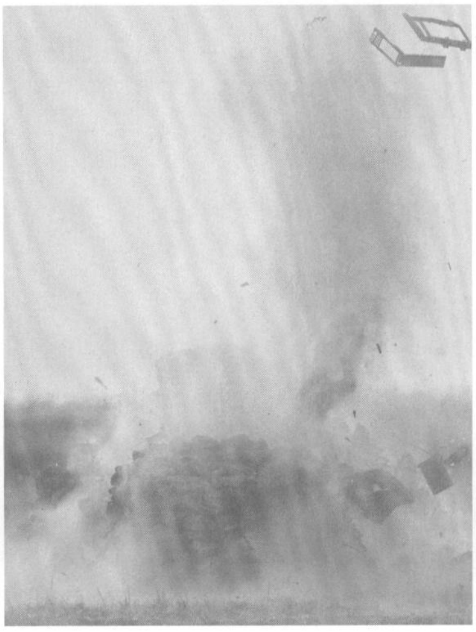

11.A

11.B

07 Film still from "I am a Human", 2022, single-channel video, 4K, color, from Death by GPS, 2022–ongoing.

08 "You're being fragmented", from Death by GPS, 2022–ongoing.

09 Film stills from "Listen to y'all, it's a sabotage", three-channel 4K video installation, color, from Death by GPS, 2022–ongoing.

10 Film stills from "Listen to y'all, it's a sabotage", three-channel 4K video installation, color, from Death by GPS, 2022–ongoing.

11 Film stills from "Listen to y'all, it's a sabotage", three-channel 4K video installation, color, from Death by GPS, 2022–ongoing.

11.C

12

13

14

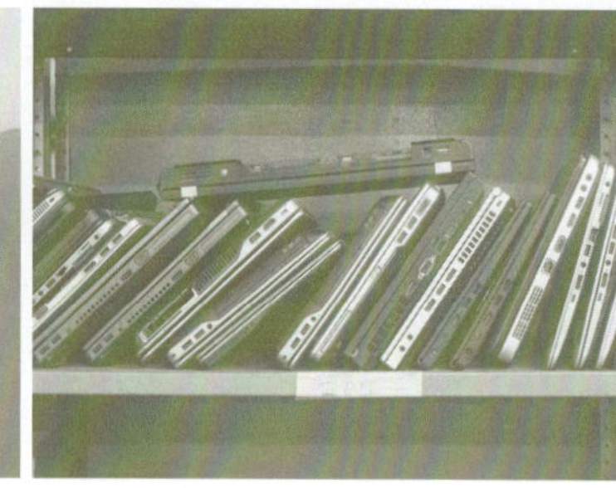

15

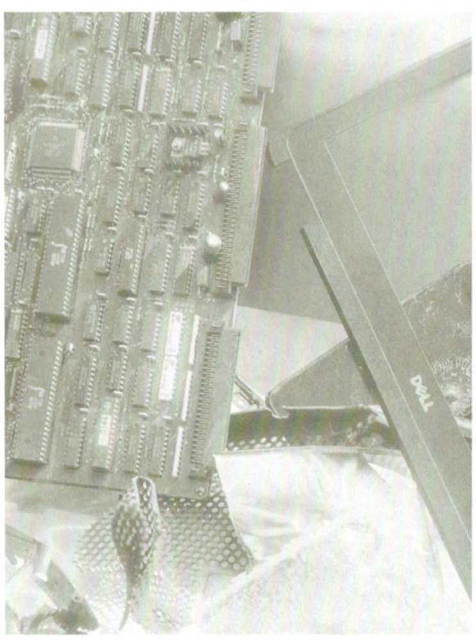

16

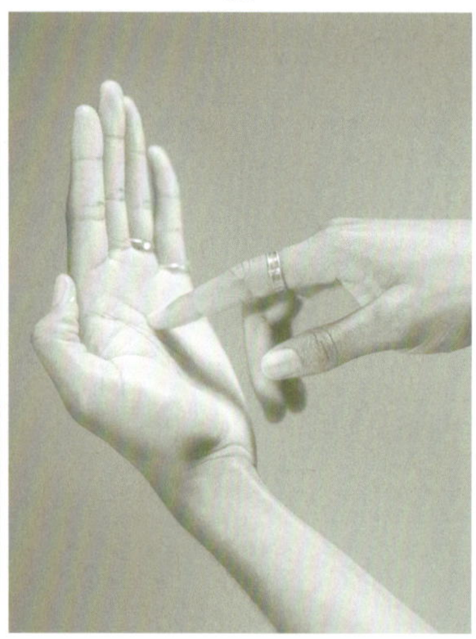

17

18

12 "A company is a group organized to create a product or service, and it is only as good as its people and how excited they are about creating." from "Death by GPS", 2022–ongoing.

13 Film still from "I am a Human", 2022, single-channel video, 4K, color, from "Death by GPS", 2022–ongoing.

14 "Adapt and expand your workforce!", from "Death by GPS", 2022–ongoing.

15 "It's getting confusing out there. Let's get organized. #2", from "Death by GPS", 2022–ongoing.

16 "Taking care of your employees is extremely important and very, very visible." from "Death by GPS", 2022-ongoing.

17 Film stills from "I am a Human", 2022, single-channel video, 4K, color, from "Death by GPS", 2022–ongoing.

18 "We're already cyborgs. Your phone and your computer are extensions of you, but the interface is through finger movements or speech, which are very slow." from "Death by GPS", 2022–ongoing.

GABRIELLA GARCIA

SEX WORK AT THE END OF THE WORLD

In 1996, Premiere Television released an instructional VHS called *How to have Cybersex on the Internet*. Our instructor is Jolie, who promises to show us "how to enjoy the stimulating world of the internet sexual playground" and "reach a cybersex climax" like "thousands of people do everyday," all while standing in front of a bucolic pond dressed in an oversized knit sweater. It's a scene devoid of anything remotely sexy while promising remote sex. "This is something I normally do in private," she titillates, "but for instructional purposes, I'm going to let you watch me have computer sex, live on the net."

What follows is about an hour of softcore porn in which we witness a now topless Jolie exploring virtual sex between internet users who have, in Jolie's words, "mastered the art of one-handed typing." The action is quite mundane: Jolie sits top-less in front of a blue screen chat room, switching between typing dirty talk and reading out the messages she receives in response. Just as with cybersex, there is no physical sexual encounter depicted in the video, even when Jolie introduces a friend, also topless, to us and her internet sexual playground. The stimulation is mediated by the screen, for Jolie and her cybersex partner, as well as for the consumers of this tape, who ostensibly purchased it for instruction.

What most fascinates me about this footage is that it *is* actually an instructional tape, hosted by a sex worker. Softcore aside, the video tells the consumer what computer hardware they need, how to hook up to the internet, and where to find others who want to engage in cybersex once they got the first two fundamentals taken care of. Premiere

Television published this VHS not for those who already had the internet, but for those who wanted to access a new type of sex.

The content of the tape reveals a historical trend at the intersection of sex and media technology. First, its promotion of new technology through seduction, featuring a most qualified professional for the job. And second, its cloaking of erotic content by way of promoting it as knowledge creation, which in this case is selling a softcore as an educational film. A century and a half before Jolie tempted us toward investing a not-insignificant amount of money to *really* get connected, the dawn of photography saw a similar pattern. According to art historian Elizabeth Anne McCauley, the first commercial photography studios found their financial footing by selling pornographic daguerreotypes, which were sold under the premise that they were *académies*, or artistic nude studies. Of course, the guise of selling photographs for the purpose of study was quite thinly veiled. "From the time of their first documented appearance in the late 1840s, photographs of the nude were sought after, collected, preserved, passed down [...] occasionally reproduced not in academic books but in limited-edition, risqué catalogues of erotica, gentlemen's guides, or brothel advertisements,"[1] McCauley writes. Costing around 20 francs at the high end (or roughly $350USD today), it was the wealthy collector who funded the success of photography, tempted into investing in new media production by the possibilities of screen-mediated virtual sex in the privacy of the home.

Paradoxically, this new freedom almost immediately contradicted itself. With each erotically-charged new media emergence comes a backlash where the medium seems to double back over on itself to become a new technology of policing. According to McCauley, the same erotic photographs that flooded the streets of Paris soon "entered into a counter-discourse constructed by criminologists and psychiatrists eager to define or punish sexual pathologies," with a growing erotica market documented by police records of studio busts and arrested photographers. Paralleling this, 1996 saw the passage of the U.S. Communications Decency Act, in response to growing fears about the ease of access to pornographic materials on the internet, about four years after it was opened to commercial interests.

As is quite obvious to anyone reading this today, the Communications Decency Act did not exactly prevent any access to internet pornography. Instead, Section 230 of the act protected internet service providers (ISPs) from liability for content that may be published on platforms by their users, as long as those providers made an effort to restrict content that was "obscene, lewd, lascivious, filthy, excessively violent, harassing, or otherwise objectionable" as defined by the US court of law. With users protected by free speech laws, this effectively made ISPs safe harbour for experimental applications of content sharing.

Jolie was therefore empowered to shepherd in an entire era of new media innovation, tempting not only new customers with her promise of digitally-accessible ecstasy, but also calling in a whole camaraderie of Jolies,

1 Anne McCauley, 'Secret Seraglios: Tracking the Female Nude in the History of Nineteenth-Century Photography', in *Histoire de l'art Du XIXe Siècle (1848–1914): Bilans et Perspectives*, ed. Claire Barbillon, Catherine Chevillon, and François-René Martin (Paris: École du Louvre, 2012).

each taking on a new experiment within the realm of the recently-possible as made true by the freedom of the internet. Jolies, supported by their monied enthusiasts, pioneered protocols for search engine optimisation, livestream video, and secure third-party payment processing. If you are the average user of the internet, this is basically Google, You-Tube, and Pay-Pal – your holy trinity of digital life. We can therefore thank the Jolies as innovators and their fans as investors for essentially ushering in the possibilities afforded to us by the popular internet as we know it today. Yet we certainly have not evolved so far from the birth of criminology to have found ourselves in a sex-positive media utopia, where Jolie is honoured for her contributions toward bringing the world closer to the democratisation of information. We are no closer to sexual liberation than those arrested for the sale of erotic photography a century ago. If history repeats itself, what counter-discourse follows the flood of digitally mediated consumer sex?

In the 25 years since this instance of media revolution, a whole industry has risen around the promise of eradicating exploitation, motivated by the hypervisibility of sex work on the internet. The Fight Online Sex Trafficking Act (FOSTA) of 2018 reinterpreted the Mann Act, a century-plus old federal law criminalising transport for the purpose of prostitution or other illegal sexual acts, to include ISPs as a method of transport. This effectively eroded the same Section 230 protections that allowed Jolie to build our internet and made it a liability for sex workers to congregate in digital space. Products of commercial sex on the internet are now evidence of crime, documented and collected by platforms who might profit off of a counter-discourse that criminalises commercially-accessed flesh.

And so, what commercial sex innovates, institutions of power use to eradicate, producing both the technology and its content to make evidence of this criminality possible. For all her effort getting people signed on so they can get off, Jolie is now a potential trafficker.

"Prisons are built with stones of law, brothels with bricks of religion." William Blake, The Marriage of Heaven and Hell

Michel Foucault argues that sexuality is not so much about the act of sex, but actually the institutionally-located discourses about sex that produced an apparatus called "sexuality", deployable as a technical machinery of control. By producing knowledge around experiences of sex – through the Christian confessional, through the psychoanalyst's chair, through the doctor's examination – a whole taxonomy of desire is born. It's not that perversion or deviance didn't exist prior, but upon this "solidification of the sexual mosaic" there became a code one could call upon to enforce restriction of movement based on expressions of sex and desire. According to Foucault, the discursive explosion only became a deployable weapon to enforce hegemony when it was threatened. "Conflicts were necessary,"Foucault says, "in order for the proletariat to be granted a body and a sexuality; economic emergencies had to arise."[2]

According to Melissa Gira Grant, the classifiable prostitute character emerged as part of this technology, transforming from a verb (*to* prostitute) to a noun (*a* prostitute) in the 19th century.[3] Grant says that this mutation of behaviour into identity created a subclass "that could now be more easily imagined, located, treated, and controlled by the law." The word "pornography" also emerged around the same time, to define the documentation, either written or illustrated, of the sale of sex. This is the historical moment when the photograph became evidence of crime. As a multiplicity of discourse on sex is "produced by a whole series of mechanisms operating in different institutions," we also saw the need to invest in media for documentation and distribution of such discourse and its counter.

Yet both Foucault's sexual mosaic and Grant's mutation are only modernist interpretations of an already deeply-seated tradition that depended on the criminalisation of the feminised body.

In *Caliban and the Witch*, Silvia Federici correlates the rise of the European witch-hunt to the General Crisis of the 17th century, a period of economic and political collapse that devastated the population. Witches were "rebel bodies" that threatened the literal production of labour-power, and they were hunted as part of a campaign to "criminalise birth control and place the female body, the uterus, at the service of population growth."[4] Definitions of witchcraft included adultery and prostitution as sites of non-productive sexuality. Given the "explosion" of prostitution that Federici documents in the 15th and 16th centuries due to the rise of mercantilism and the expelling of peasant women from commonwealth labour as land became privatised, these new laws led to the massacring of hundreds of thousands of women who were either unwilling or unable to achieve "fixed reproductive work" as full-time housewives.

Thus, Federici argues that Foucault's disciplining of the body could only arise after over *two hundred years* of state terrorism that "destroyed a whole world of female practices, collective relations and systems of knowledge that had been the foundation of women's power in pre-capitalist Europe." Similar to the rise of the photograph as evidence, Federici notes that the rise of the witch-hunt coincides with the nascence of demographic recording and its resultant possibility of granting power to the state in the supervision of sexuality, procreation, and family life.

The imprisonable (or executable) mutation therefore occurs around cultural crisis or flux, and always with new technologies of information-sharing. It is as though the sex worker rises from the rubble of any tectonic social shift. The prostitute embodies the fear of hegemonic collapse, of disorder, of revolt.

A "demurring" Jolie invited us into her living room in 1996. The early 1990s marked the peak of American global

2 Miche Foucault, *The History of Sexuality: An Introduction* (New York: Random House, 1978).

3 Melissa Gira Grant, *Playing the whore: the work of sex work* (New York: Verso, 2014).

4 Silvia Federici, *Caliban and the Witch: Women, the Body and Primitive Accumulation* (New York: Autonomedia, 2004).

hegemony. The Cold War "ended" and the Wall fell. The economy was booming, and cultural exchange centred the United States like a pool reflecting the visage of Narcissus. A new information technology was born, and in 1994 the internet became a global marketplace for the exchange of (generally American) ideas and trade. Of course Jolie was happy there – not a threat to the status quo, she was a seductress to all things that brought the world closer to capital F Freedom.

Now Jolie has mutated into a trafficker. Her actions never changed, but the world around her did. The infrastructure of the internet – popularised, funded and designed by erotic labour – snaked its way quite literally into your pants toward ubiquity, epitomised by the smartphone. Melissa Gira Grant notes that open access to the internet made sex work a viable option for those who would have never previously considered the trade when it was physically cordoned off into localised spaces of impropriety ("red light" districts). This made it "possible for many people to try out sex work, organised online and conducted in private without risking becoming a known prostitute." By moving to the private sphere of the digital, engagement in sex trades could go undetected, dismantling "conventional ways we'd distinguish a prostitute from a non-prostitute woman." Simultaneously, the West faced multiple crises that threatened its hold on the hegemony, each a new opportunity to engineer a shadow whore toward which to direct a strangling moral panic.

When the 2008 financial crisis plunged millions into unemployment, the line distinguishing prostitute from non-prostitute blurred into oblivion as many turned to a sort of obfuscated erotic labour to make ends meet. This was especially attractive to students who had accumulated trillions of dollars of university loan debt before being turned out into a catastrophic job market. In 2010, Seeking Arrangement, a "sugar baby" website which promised to connect "attractive partners" seeking "mutually beneficial" relationships, began offering free premium memberships to sugar babies who registered using their university email addresses. This resulted in a 58 per cent increase in college enrolees to an already large pool of sugar babies and their daddies who were quickly accepting this new form of financially-motivated dating as plausibly-deniable erotic trade. Similarly, Jeff Davids, the founder of now-shuttered male escort site RentBoy.com, reported a surge of "new and interesting escorts in 2009," saying "people who were laid off their cushy $200,000 year Merrill Lynch jobs and had the gym memberships and the nice clothes looked in the mirror and said, 'I'm going to be an escort, and it's going to be more fun.'"

The (ongoing) series of crises brought upon us by the Covid-19 pandemic only confirmed the phenomenon. All the lockdowns in the world could not wipe sex work from the face of the planet: instead, the possibilities of selling sexual content online became one of the few no-contact options for income as employers around the world shut their businesses down indefinitely. Less than a month into the total lockdown of New York City, *The New York Times* reported a major increase in digital sex work, noting that trade-facilitating platforms experienced spikes in sign-ups. OnlyFans, for instance, disclosed 3.7 million new accounts created between March 1 and

April 10, 2020. Independent adult content sharing had finally entered the realm of casual online gig work, troubling definitions of sex work so thoroughly that the prostitute construct may just about be showing its slip. When in December 2020 the *New York Post* tried to publicly shame a paramedic for her participation on OnlyFans to make up for lost income during the pandemic, New York congresswoman Alexandria Ocasio-Cortez defended the woman saying, "the actual scandalous headline here is 'Medics in the United States need two jobs to survive.'"

We are now experiencing a particular period in which the sex worker holds enormous value in the political economy, within the context of technological innovation-to-elimination pipeline. A new discursive explosion was fed by user-generated media in the years leading up to our current state of "whorephobic" policy that places the internet in its crosshairs. The casual visibility of sex work through adult service ads on classifieds sites such as Craigslist or Backpage "evidenced" a supposed scourge of sex trafficking, despite no quantitative research backing this claim (in fact, reports of sex trafficking would actually increase *after* aforementioned FOSTA laws decimated sex worker-friendly spaces on the internet). The walled-garden internet became a panopticon's Eden, ripe for the collecting, tagging, parsing, and categorising of extractable data. Places where sex workers congregated online became object-models upon which surveillance machine learning technologies could train toward algorithmic identification of prostitute versus non-prostitute. Is it a coincidence that these digital spaces served to re-establish female practices, collective relations and systems of knowledge, much like those disposed of by Europe's gynocidal massacres studied by Federici?

All of this occurs against the backdrop of the West's greatest failure to protect its domination. A mere decade after securing its position as the singular global empire with the 1991 dissolution of the Soviet Union, the attacks on 9/11 showed just how fragile such status could be. The answer according to the United States was to couple an anti-terrorism campaign with a promise to eradicate human trafficking. According to legal scholar Ratna Kapur, the sex worker as "victimised subject is based on the assumptions of the 'other' as incapable of self-determination, justifying rescue and rehabilitation operations."[5] This argued a moral obligation allowing the US to justify technology-driven surveillance of other nation-states under the premise of victim rescue. The US therefore begins to use the second discursive explosion as evidenced by the visibility of sex work on the internet to push for "imperialist interventions in the form of antitrafficking legislation and intensified moral surveillance" that control the migration of bodies through space in order to assert its power.

What is it about these accelerationist moments of information technology that seems to centre the whore? Why does she suddenly become so visible – as a pathfinder for innovation and movement, as vector of disease and pathology, as a dualistic icon of feminine agency and exploited victim?

The most jaded, conspiratorial folks would argue that surveillance-based governmentalities *allowed* sex work to exist online for so long specifically to feed this mechanism of control. But for all that affordance, it also allowed for the demystification and "gentrification" of sex work, as we saw in the explosion of its participants during Western world-shattering crises. It's a sort of ratcheting effect: each time a supremacist system takes a swing at sex work, it grows in power like a hydra. Ironically, sex work would have likely remained in the shadows had it not been for these new punitive social and technological interventions. Sex work as a construct is in fact antifragile, gaining from shock, volatility, and noise. And somehow this gives me hope.

In all my research on sex work and technology, there is a constant dedication to creating a taxonomy that ignores the consent or the experience of the individual as just existing in a set of circumstances presented to them upon birth. Can I reverse-engineer the technology of coding prostitution, strip the behaviour from its place as an identity, and try to better understand the mutation itself as the true object of inquiry? If all this was born of modernity's addiction to a logical measure of progress, what happens if we instead hold the mutation and observe its role as a phenomenon that seems to crop up at sites where cultural shift meets advancements in mass media development? If the hegemony insists on creating a shadow whore, can we free her of her exploitation by governmentalities of discipline? Anna Tsing uses patchiness, or "a mosaic of open-ended assemblages of entangled ways of life," and how disrupted ecosystems are fertile grounds for studying a third nature, or what may thrive *because of* precarity, despite the ruins of progressive industrial capitalism.[6] For us to do so, we must embrace indeterminacy, the "unplanned nature of time," which might allow us to see how we are shaped by encounter or "shifting assemblages". Indeterminacy resists mechanised regimes of order. In their exploration of the relationship between classification and indeterminacy, Catherine Alexander and Andrew Sanchez look toward indeterminacy "as a mode of potentiality, resistance, escape, creativity, and improvisation" so that "people can reimagine their own futures."[7]

I want to walk through the patchiness of assemblages which seem to *need* the sex worker "element" to design order. While a multinational public-private partnership manufactures the shadow whore toward her eradication, she has simultaneously solidified as an act of defiance. I want to bring forth a teleology of sex work, which in purpose reveals constructs of control. The sex worker *is* indeterminacy. She is a morphology in and of herself, shapeshifting constantly in order to survive. She exists beyond theory, while at the same time she acts as a mirror to the socio-political construct of any given epoch. Conjuring the shadow whore is in fact the flagging of a weakened supremacy, backed into a corner by its own failure to make good on promises of progress.

Perhaps there is even space to bring this indeterminacy even further. We have seen crises obscure the line be-

5 Ratna Kapur, 'Post-Colonial Economies of Desire: Legal Representations of the Sexual Subaltern.' *Denver University Law Review* 78, no. 4 855–886 (Denver, CO, 2001).

tween prostitute and non-prostitute. What happens therefore when it is no longer possible to detect the difference at all? Sylvia Federici might argue that this could lay the groundwork for a new witch-hunt, in which the accusation alone could be enough for *any* body to be criminalised. Melissa Gira Grant might say that this would help support the term "sex work" as itself an act of semiotic resistance, by transitioning the mutated prostitute identity back from "a state of being to a form of labour," so that the "designation of sex work is the invention of those who perform it." I can imagine this indeterminacy as a virus, a glitch with the potential to break any system based on taxonomy. When everyone's a whore, no one is a whore. We are all just trying to get by.

Sometimes I picture myself a whore, pushed up against the precipice of modernity. Whose instrument of measurement am I, truly? Who actually fucks me, and who benefits from my fucking? Do I get to choose, or am I just a hole in history? Perhaps I am exploiting industrialism and my newfound ability to run away, because I would be a slave-wife or dead otherwise. Perhaps I am the product of Empire, where I inadvertently support the colonial project because I see my own independence in the big bucks I'll earn by making pioneertown hospitable. Perhaps I give birth to laws, which apparently might save me. Perhaps I'm an orphan of existence, whore-bastard, bastard-whore with a future predetermined by something so alien, that I can't help but feel invaded. I have found a way to live, but theory won't leave me alone.

I try to shed the preconceived notions of my place in history, as though any author has truly been able to capture my experience.

I think of myself outside of the constraints of a political economy, as an existing creature who must go on, with all the wits she has gathered. Who likes to fuck. Who likes to move.

I avoid historiography as a fox would avoid a trap, recognizing that the caught fox has no story to tell when the trap has evidenced its win.

What is it like to have a criminalized stigma descend upon me? Like watching a bomb drop from a mystery, to cover my being with meaning. Can it be so simple, this draping of identity? Is there space for me, who never chose to be a subject, but is inevitably politicized without consent?

This is where theory betrays the fact of the matter, which is that bodies will innovate to survive regardless of the myriad philosophies or technologies of control that may arise at any given time.

6 Anna Lowenhaupt Tsing, *The Mushroom at the End of the World* (Princeton, N.J: Princeton University Press, 2017).

7 Catherine Alexander, and Andrew Sanchez, *Indeterminacy: Waste, Value, and the Imagination*, WYSE Series in Social Anthropology 7 (New York: Berghahn Books, 2019).

LISE STR

THE ALPH

202

ATSMA

STRATEG

203

Y

204

Self-help, Do-it-Yourself, YouTube tutorials and wikiHow. From apprenticeship and peer-to-peer transmitted knowledge to bookshop categories and internet forums, the information age has turned know-how, savviness, and techniques into yet another heap of data that one hoards. Why does one hoard—objects, or information? For security? Comfort? Reassurance? To cope with anxiety?

The series "Alpha Strategy" by photographer Lise Straatsma is not about bunkers and survivalists but about how one copes with fear, and our relation to information overload. In Straatsma's words, her project is about "how to regain control and weapon yourself against anxiety." At the core of preppers or survivalist communities—a social movement actively getting ready for cataclysmic events—lies profound anxiety for an unpredictable future. The result of this fear might be pre-emptive isolation—retreating to the most remote parts of one's country, trusting only the most immediate members of your community while rejecting any external intervention. But the people and the infrastructure Straatsma photographed offer a very different perspective. More than the stereotypical typology of the bunker, or the neat accumulation of food rations, her project focuses on preppers' knowledge build-up.

Is knowledge power or is ignorance bliss? Fear is a highly useful emotion that has been preserved throughout evolution to secure humanity's survival. People say we fear what we do not know. Gaining more knowledge should technically make us less fearful. But the more you know, the more you understand what you do not know. Will the anticipation of the unknown by the accumulation of knowledge bring reassurance or fuel fear?

XXL
Basmati

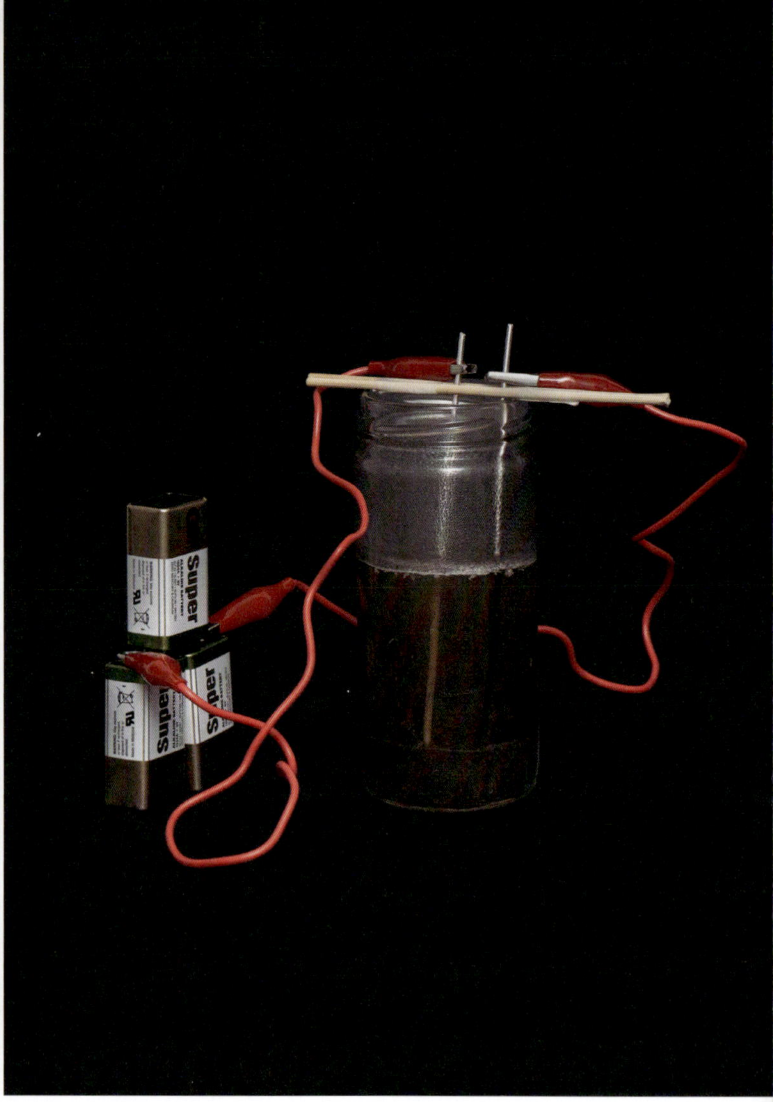
Super
Super
Super

PARIS
Fly
Emirates

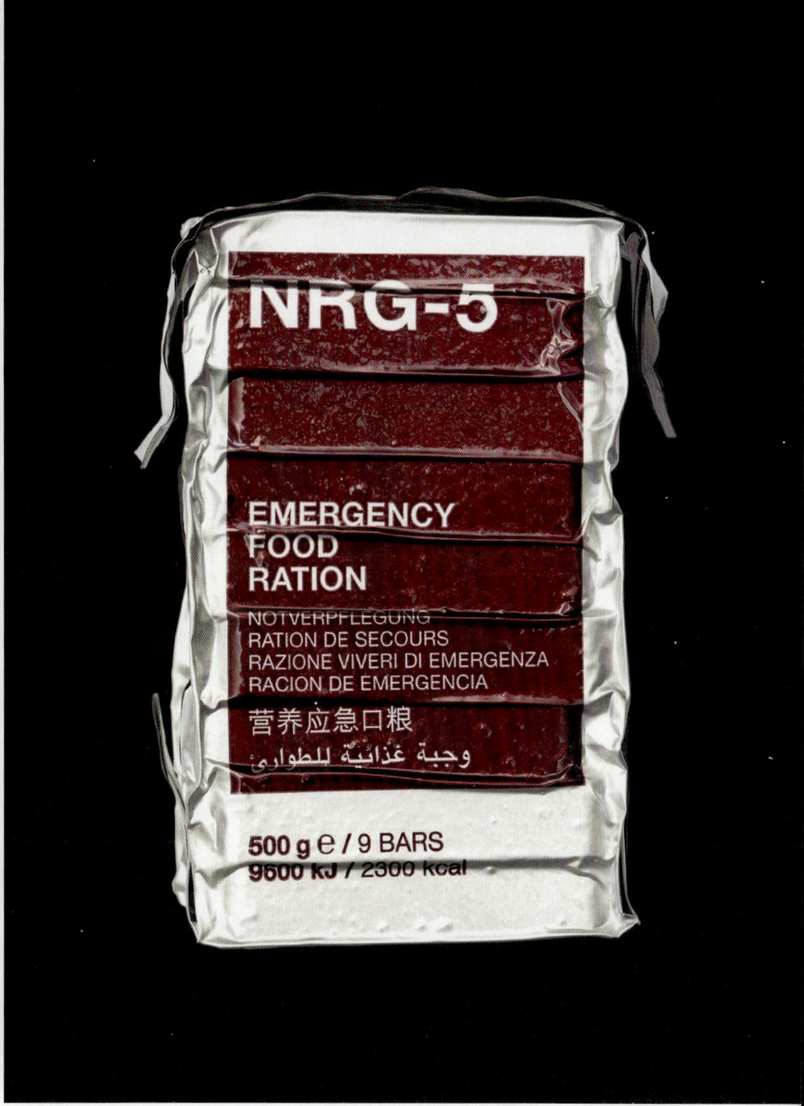
NRG-5
EMERGENCY
FOOD
RATION
NOTVERPFLEGUNG
RATION DE SECOURS
RAZIONE VIVERI DI EMERGENZA
RACION DE EMERGENCIA
营养应急口粮
وجبة غذائية للطوارئ
500 g ℮ / 9 BARS
9600 kJ / 2300 kcal

2002

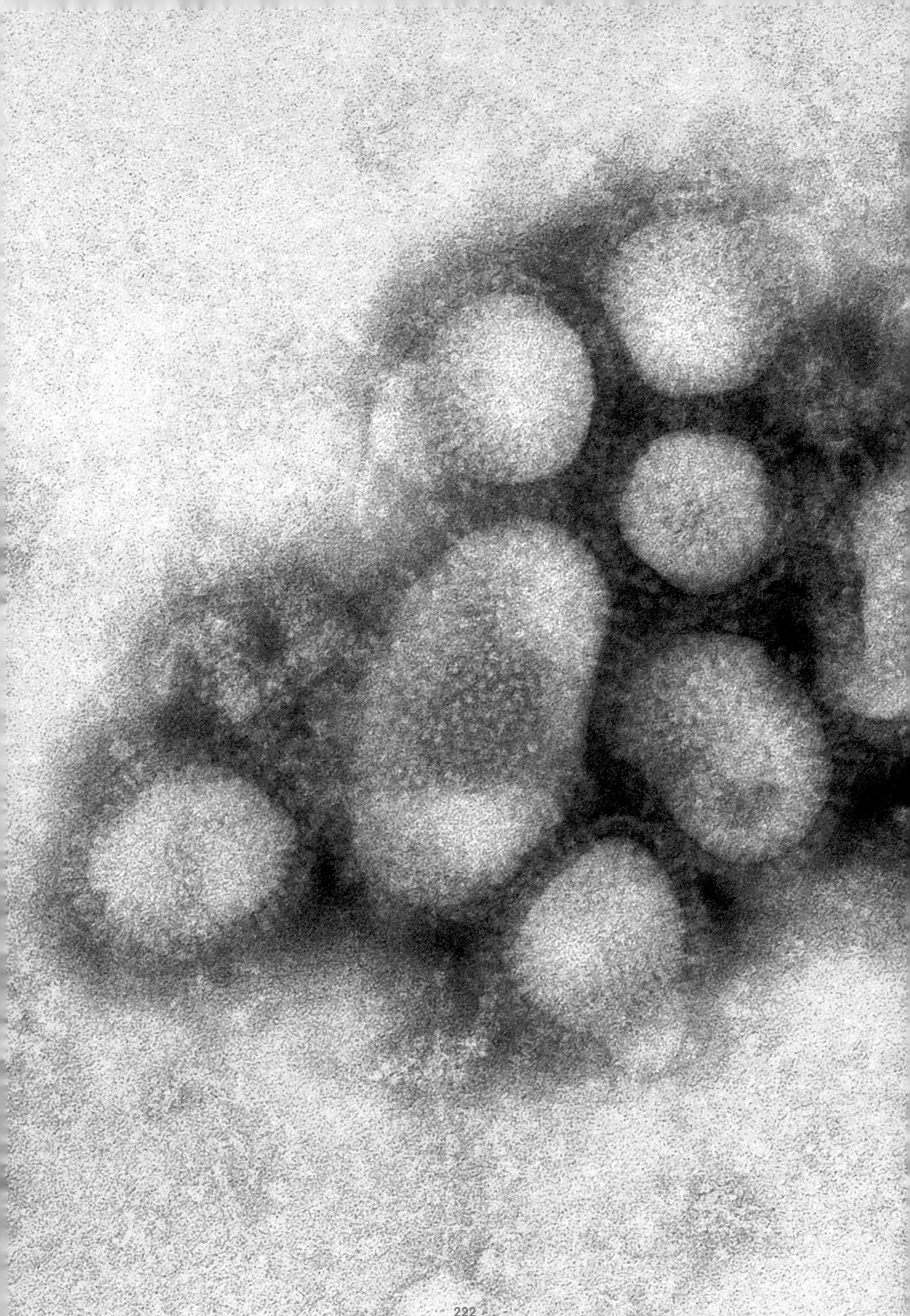

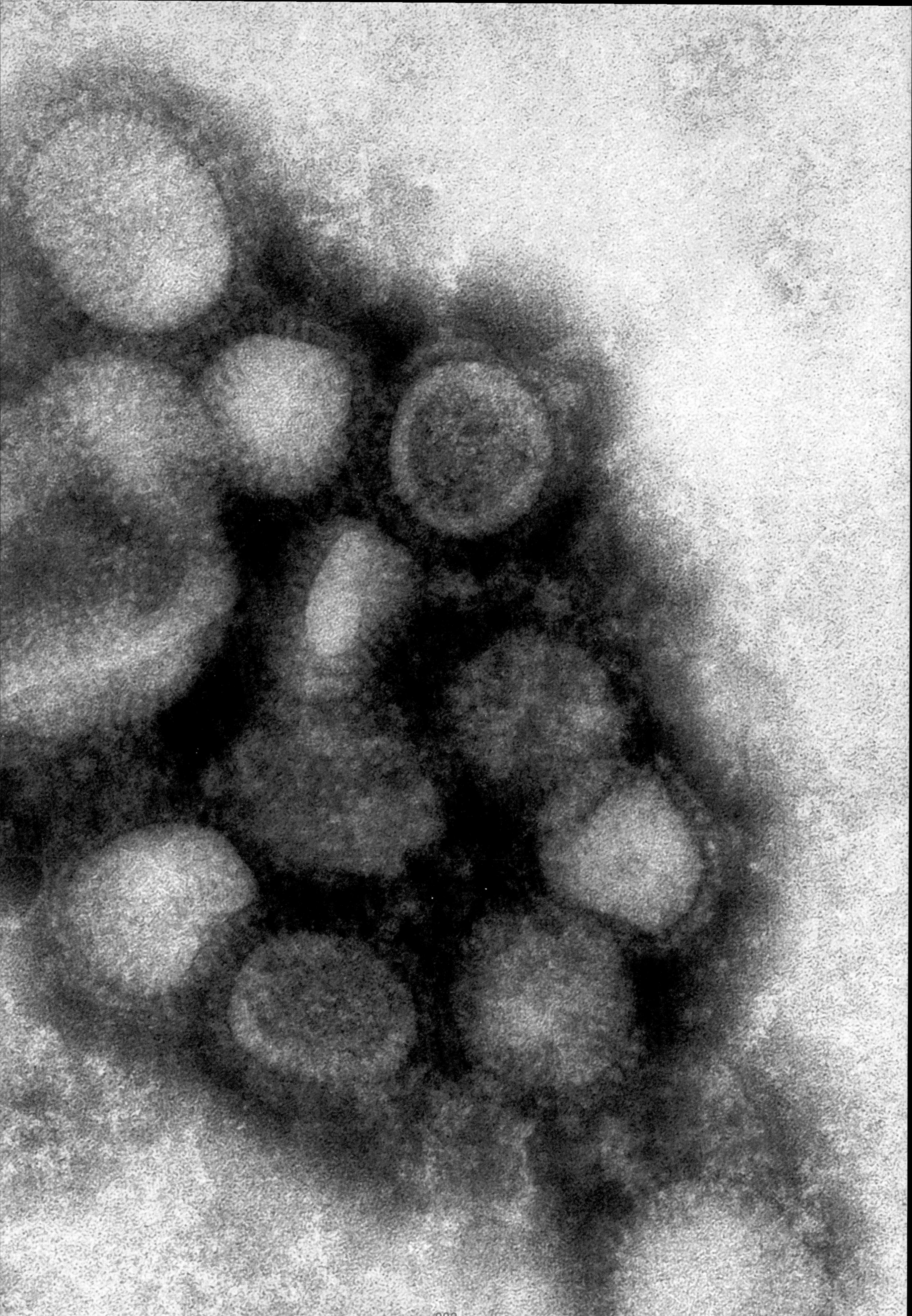

HELLA
unox
Stevige Tomaten soep
Struik
COQUETTE
Erwten-Soep
met rookworst

01

02

03

04

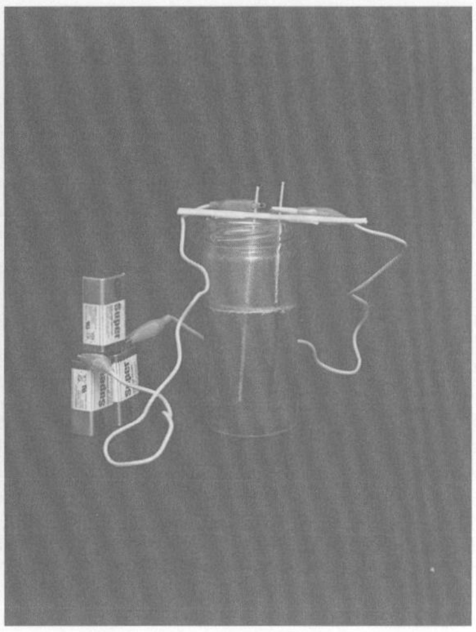

01 Storage area in Nander's house, 2016. "It's actually not that strange to have a few bottles of water in your house."

02 Storage containers in Steffen's house, 2016. "If you prep seriously, you don't just tell everyone of course. Because then everybody will come to your house if something happens."

03 Homemade water filtration system containing cloth, sand, gravel and activated charcoal.

04 Homemade colloidal silver (said to have similar attributes as antibiotics, but scientifically disputed).

05

06

07

08

09

10

11

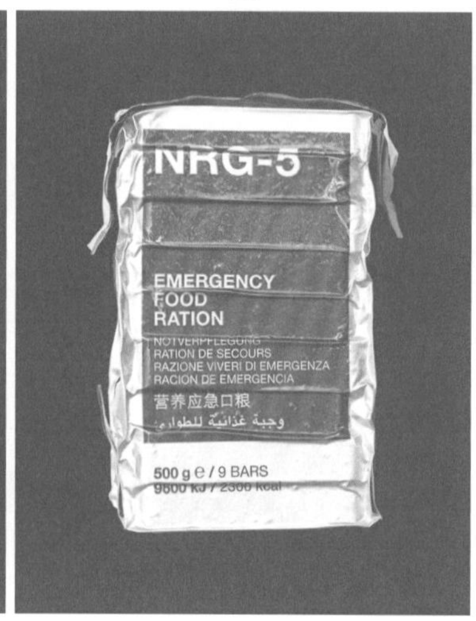

12

05 Steffen, 2016. "It would be weird if we die without experiencing war. Historically that doesn't happen in Europe. Our parents were the first to experience that. So there is no reason to be sure this will continue."
06 Mushroom cloud of the atomic bomb dropped on Hiroshima (code name: '"Little boy"), killing an estimated 140,000 people both as a direct result of the blast and from later radiation sickness. Photographed by the US army. Source: Hiroshima Peace Memorial Museum.
07 Berts bedroom, 2016. "I have become older and am definitely not afraid of dying. That's not the reason behind it [preparing]. People tend to think I live in fear every day but this is definitely not the case."
08 Nuclear bunker built by the Dutch Department of Defence during the Cold War, in 1979. It was built in a hill mainly consisting of marl, known for its air purifying qualities, 2016.
09 Bert, 2016. "People take for granted that we have water coming from our taps, when this is not a given."
10 Homemade light source containing water, tin foil, toilet paper and sunflower oil.
11 Store bought emergency food ration.
12 North Sea Flood, 1953. The flood struck the Netherlands (1836 deaths), England (307 deaths) and Belgium (28 deaths). Another 244 lives were lost at sea. Overnight more than 400,000 acres of land were covered in water. Source: "Rijkswaterstaat".

13

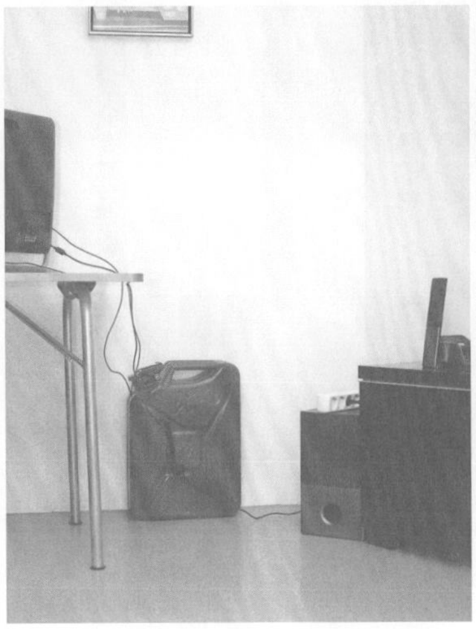

14

15

16

17

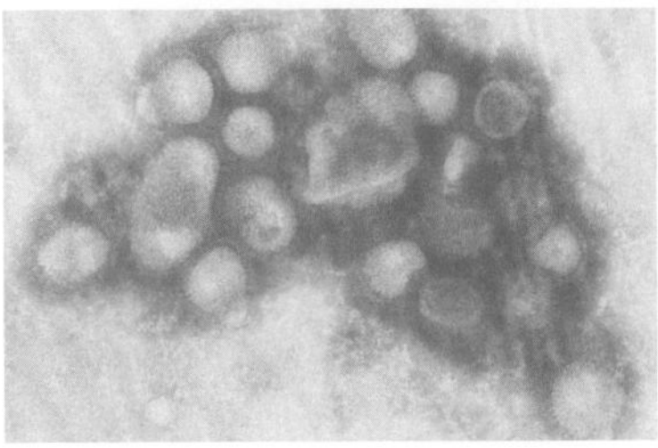

18

13 Storage container for fluids in Steffen's house, 2016.
14 Backup power generators. Reinier de Graaf hospital, 2016.
15 Nander, 2016. "Russia could tell us they are cutting off the gas supply. You then would want to have some things in your house. Everything is fragile."
16 Storage area in Bert's house, 2016. "The most tragic thing I can think of is when you, as a prepper, succumb to your own preps. If petroleum leaks onto your tile floor, there is no direct danger. A spark would instantly fade out. This however would not be the case on a carpet floor. Petroleum containers are safe when kept in a bathtub."
17 Microscopic image of influenza A virus, subtype H1N1. Commonly known as the Spanish flu, one of the deadliest known natural disasters in human history. Source: Public Health Image Library, Centre for Disease Control and Prevention.
18 Storage area in Berts house, 2016. "My sister, who is also a prepper but a more moderate one, always mentions the umbrella. She says: "I prep so nothing will happen". The thing about carrying an umbrella is that you take it with to hopefully ward off the rain."

MATTHIEU

VIVANTS

228

GAFSOU

229

ANXIETY BLURRED BOUNDARIES COLLAPSE DEVIANCE FRANCE FORESTS LOCKDOWN PETROL CULTURE SWITZERLAND TIRED BODIES

"Vivants", the plural of *alive* in French, is a profound and intimate series by Swiss photographer Matthieu Gafsou. It explores an eroding world and our position—as individual(s), as humankind—within this process. When we first talked to Gafsou about this series in 2019, its working title was "solastalgia", a concept coined by philosopher Glenn Albrecht in 2005 that describes the melancholia or distress caused by climate change, and our inability—individually and collectively—to act upon it. As he continued working on this project for four years, Gafsou built on concepts such as Albrecht's solastalgia but let feelings and emotions express themselves more openly: anxiety, love, anger. Chinese whales stranded in playgrounds, riots in France, portraits of his children in the Swiss countryside, modified landscapes—this series by Gafsou is at the same time dark and luminous, it is the warmth of the campfire that comforts the body in the cold night and lightens the gathering, but it is also the wounded flesh scared with scorch marks.

To the deep blacks, sanguine reds, and viridian greens, Gafsou has added the anxious iridescence of crude oil, with which he has manipulated some of the prints, crossing the boundaries of photography and taking a firm step into other forms of bricolage artmaking. In doing so, he turns the polluted skies of the city into pearly heavens, an ambivalent evocation of our conflicted relationship to infrastructural landscape that we make and destroy at the same time. Gafsou's "Vivants", dominated by night-time shots and darkness, will make your blood curdle and warm your heart at the same time, a deeply personal take on the world he lives in, and the mess we are all part of.

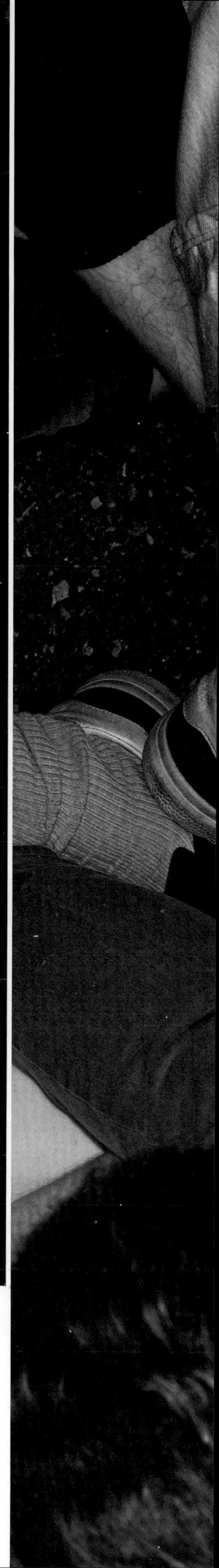

CHERISH THE
PALE BLUE DOT

DECATHLON

01

02

03

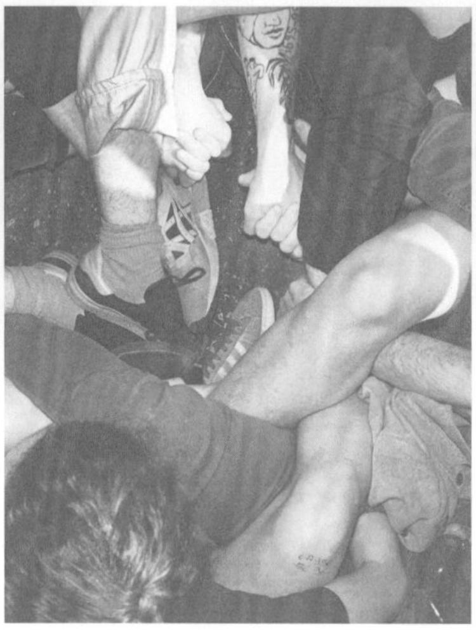

04

05

06

07

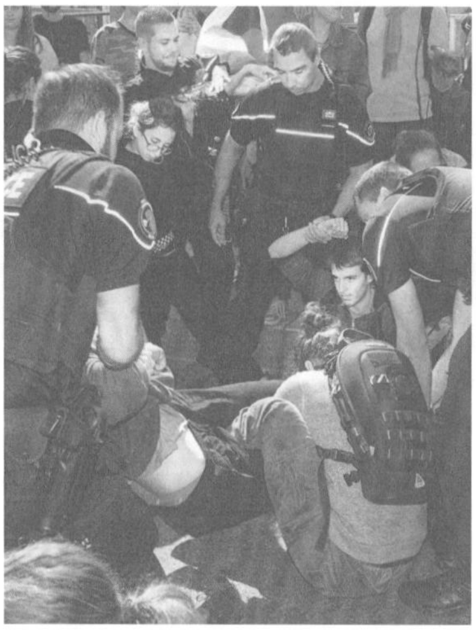

08

01 Plaie IV, 2014 (Grangettes Natural Reserve, Switzerland).
02 Vitali, 2020 (Gorges of the Jogne, Switzerland).
03 Colère XIX, 2019 (demonstration Extinction Rebellion, Lausanne, Switzerland).
04 Mafate, 2021 (La Réunion, France).
05 Volcan I, 2021 (inside the Piton de la Fournaise, La Réunion, France).
06 Zoo I, 2019 (some king penguins, *Aptenodytes patagonicus*, Zurich zoo, Switzerland).
07 Tempête II, 2015 (Lausanne).
08 Colère I, 2019 (demonstration Extinction Rebellion, Lausanne, Switzerland).

09

10

11

12

13

14

15

16

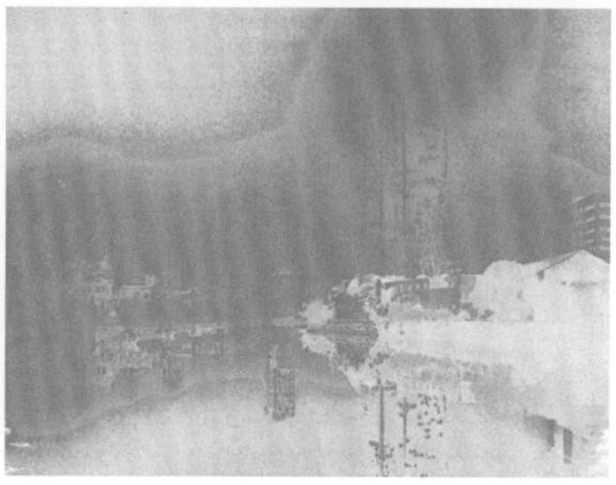

17

09 Colère X, 2020 (Climate Strike, Lausanne, Switzerland).
10 Feu II, 2019 (modified landscape).
11 Feu I, 2019 (modified landscape).
12 Errantes, 2018 (Xiamen, China).
13 Tempête I, 2020 (towards Trient, Switzerland).
14 Pétrole XVII, 2020
(inkjet prints layered with crude oil then scanned).
15 Pétrole XIV, 2020
(inkjet prints layered with crude oil then scanned).
16 Pétrole V, 2020
(inkjet prints layered with crude oil then scanned).
17 Pétrole XI, 2020
(inkjet prints layered with crude oil then scanned).

JUSTINIEN TRIBILLON

INVENTING INFRASTRUCTURE

An etymological blueprint

Explosions. Damn collapsing. An airfield caving in as an airplane takes off. Cars crashing in the abyss from an elevated highway coming apart. Typhoons and earthquakes. Aliens. Heroes wreaking havoc on their quest for justice. Terrorists. Terrorists. Terrorists.

> "Infrastructure," explains comedian John Oliver, "it's our roads, bridges, dams, levies, airports, power-grids. Basically, anything that can be destroyed in an action movie. […] If an alien species judged humanity by our most popular movies, they'd think we're furious with asphalt all the time."

A technical jargon apparently borrowed from development economics, the *Oxford Dictionary* defines infrastructure as "the basic physical and organisational structures and facilities needed for the operation of a society or enterprise." A Google search for "infrastructure" returns 5.6 billion results; a search on the same term in the news section of the same engine gives 163 million occurrences. An immensely popular jargon, then.

"Infrastructure" is a popular expression because it is evocative: it encapsulates modernity – the association of capital, statal project, and technology. Arguably, we collectively share a networked imaginary where our social and economic structures rest on a series of interdependent systems that enable them to function: the roads and rail tracks that bring us to work in the morning, the internet and mobile networks that allow us to watch Netflix on our laptops, our power-grids, and water pipes.

"Infrastructure" has morphed to become sociotechnical metonymy. This metonymic might is why the Morandi bridge collapsing in Genoa was not only the tragic downfall of a viaduct but also that of an Italian national myth.[1] This metonymic might is why the screenwriters for Hollywood "blockbuster" movies never miss a chance to burn down roads, bridges, dams, levies, airports, power-grids. Infrastructures are symbols and supports of social imagination. As Roland Barthes would say, they are myths that act as signs.

And yet, we barely know how the word came to be. We do not know how it was born. We barely know when. We have no critical understanding as to why it emerged – why did we need "infrastructure" when "network" had been around for centuries? We live in an "infrastructural age"[2] but there is no comprehensive research on the word's etymological, cultural, and critical journey. More than any other words, "infrastructure" is a political project that defines our relationship to technology, capital, colonisation, resources extraction. Let us unearth the concept's intellectual roots to understand the world built on this image.

Fourteen letters and nine consonants. The word's pronunciation, in English especially, is so difficult that the Internet offers countless video tutorials explaining how to correctly go about enunciating ˈɪnfrəstrʌktʃə.

"Infrastructure" is a calque from French. A calque, or loan translation, is "an expression adopted by one language from another in a more or less literally translated form."[3] It belongs to a long list of words borrowed from French and brought into the English lexicon in the early 20th century – such as "limousine", "fuselage", "supersonic". "Infrastructure" does not have the ancient history of apparent synonyms like "network" (16th century in English, 15th century for the French *réseau*) that I have already mentioned. Nor was it invented to name a new technological invention such as the computer: *ordinateur* in French but often a calque word from English in other languages, e.g. *computadora* in Spanish, *computer* in Dutch and German, *компьютер* ("komp'-yúter") in Russian. As a calque, "infrastructure" exists in pretty much the same form and same meaning in an endless list of languages across different families, most especially Indo-European. *Infrastruktur* (German), *infraestructura* (Spanish), *infrastruttura* (Italian), *infrastructuur* (Dutch), but also *инфраструктура* ("infrastruktura", Russian). And of course, *infrastructure* in French.

At the outset, one can therefore emit three hypotheses when considering this similarity across different languages. (a) That "infrastructure" is a recent word; (b) that "infrastructure" is a technical term that was transmitted across languages via technical and

1 Guglielmo Mattioli, 'What Caused the Genoa Bridge Collapse—and the End of an Italian National Myth?', *The Guardian* (26 February 2019). https://www.theguardian.com/cities/2019/feb/26/what-caused-the-genoa-morandi-bridge-collapse-and-the-end-of-an-italian-national-myth.

2 Wendy Steele, and Crystal Legacy, 'Critical Urban Infrastructure', *Urban Policy and Research* 35, no. 1 (2 January 2017), 1–6.

3 'Loan Translation', in *The Oxford Dictionary of English Grammar* (Oxford: Oxford University Press, 2014).

specialist literature; (c) that it was adopted extremely quickly (within decades, if not years) by these different languages and via very specific semantic channels (e.g. an industry, a political network, a trade – which indeed takes us back to the second hypothesis).

The birth of "infrastructure" took place in two steps. The concept came first, the word only second.

On 11 June 1842, King Louis Philippe of France signed a bill of law to stimulate the expansion of railway across the country and indeed Europe. France was lagging well behind the United Kingdom, whose railway industry was thriving, emboldened by the Railway Mania. The bill delivered what we would call today a strategic design for the expansion of railway across France, listing out the connections to be built in the coming years. The star-shaped design with Paris in its centre, known as *Étoile de Legrand* after the engineer who conceived it, still organises France's railway network today.

More than the expression of a spatial project, the bill also looked at addressing what was then perceived as the biggest handicap for French railway expansion: money, or lack thereof. The bill did so by devising an interesting double dichotomy, above/below and private/public, here to stimulate the financing and building of new railway lines. Indeed, the bill decreed that the State and local authorities would bear the following costs: land acquisition, levelling, erection of bridges and opening of tunnels. On the other hand, private operators were to pay for the installation of railway tracks, the cost of exploitation and maintenance, the purchase and repair of rolling stocks. In a nutshell: the cost of what sat *below* the railway tracks was to be borne by the "public sector" (forgive this anachronism), the tracks and what sat *above* was the domain of private actors.

Since the 1820s and the successful coupling of railway and steam technologies—the premise of a revolution in rail transport – the financing, modes of exploitation, maintenance of railway lines had led to heated debates amongst intellectuals, politicians, and industrialists. The development of railway brought fundamental economic and political challenges – which to a certain extent remain debated today – on profitability, the possibility of balancing the cost of construction and the cost of exploitation, but also on the statute of railway workers, their rights and duties, etc. At the core of this complex discussion was the issue of *if* and *how* should the State intervene.

Commentators also started to understand the revolutionary impact of modern railway on humanity's relationship to space and time. They started to understand that the world would be changed forever. In 1852, prominent intellectual and political figure Michel Chevalier (1806–1879) envisioned that

> *The European will have an estate in New Zealand or Australia, the same way 200 years ago a French lord had land in Provence and an English baron a castle in Scotland. Two friends, parting in Paris, will set their next meeting in Calcutta or Mexico, without finding this the least extraordinary. […] From Rome to Edinburgh, we will be neighbours. […] And the*

wise will understand that instead of being shrunk and belittled, our planet will then be fecundated.[4]

To fully grasp the historical context, it is also crucial to bear in mind that this technological invention and the debates on its development and implementation took place within an ebullient "long" 19th century: between 1800 and 1870, France would go through seven different political regimes (namely three republics, two empires, two monarchies). Countless political-cum-philosophical movements, sects and factions emerged and fought – metaphorically and often physically. Amongst them, the immensely influential followers of Henri de Saint-Simon.

Saint-Simonianism was a complex intellectual movement born in the first half of the 19th century. Named after Henri Vouvroy de Saint-Simon (1760–1825), its core ideology rested on the belief that technological progress would change society for the better, bringing happiness, emancipation, and freedom. Saint-Simon's thought is commonly identified as a form of utopian socialism with its intellectual foundations in 18th century French materialist philosophy. After Saint-Simon's death, the movement stemmed into different sects – including an influential church led by Prosper Enfantin (1796–1864) – that promoted varied readings of Saint-Simon's thought. Karl Marx (1818–1883) and Friedrich Engels (1820–1895) considered Saint-Simon as one of the most influential intellectuals of socialism. Yet somehow confusingly (from our contemporary point of view), the Count of Saint-Simon was also the flagship thinker for proponents of free-trade and capitalism. In various forms, and supported by miscellaneous stakeholders, Saint-Simon's ideas were significantly present in 19th century Europe and especially France, most especially amongst its elites (engineers, economists, intellectuals, capitalists), those that were not yet called technocrats.

Amongst these foremost figures of Saint-Simonianism were Emile (1800–1875) and Isaac Pereire (1806–1880). The Brothers Pereire were then some of the most powerful bankers in Europe and key actors in the railway industry, in France and abroad. In an epic competition between Europe's most powerful bankers and politicians that took place in 1856–1857, the syndicate they led won the mandate to found Russia's main railway company. In typical Saint-Simonian fashion, the Pereires' ambition in financing and laying the tracks of European railways was a mix of financial gain, resources extraction and "civilisational" project by way of technological "progress". As Isaac Pereire wrote to this brother in July 1856: "We are going to develop a virgin territory whose hinterland, to some degree unexplored, contains enormous natural resources. It is only necessary to link up the productive centres with the ports of the country in order to extract products which will spare Europe from (any) scarcity."[5]

The legal document (written in French) signed between Alexander II of Russia and the consortium led by the Brothers Pereire, that marked the foundation of the Great Company of Russian Railways in January 1857 used for the first time the term *infrastructure* and the dualism *infrastructure/superstructure*. *Infra-*, the Latin for below; *super-* (or *supra-*) for

4 Michel Chevalier, *Chemins de fer* (Paris: Guillaumin, 1852), 13–14.

above. This is the first ever mention of *infrastructure* I could find in French. It espouses the definition established in 1842. The same year, a newspaper used for the first time the word "infrastructure" to report the creation of the Russian Railway Company.

This dualism between what was below the railway and funded by the State, and what sat above and financed by private actors established in the law of 1842 had now acquired names of their own: *infrastructure* and *superstructure*. Rarely used and never applied to railway before, "superstructure" is a term that had existed since the 17th century. In French and in English, it describes the superfluous element of a building, a play, a book and is used by Voltaire in 1764 for instance. However, I have found no evidence that "infrastructure" existed, at all, in any form and in any language, before this mention in 1857.

It is also interesting to note that, the opposition infrastructure/superstructure does not come from engineering *per se*, but from its financing. Infrastructure is the invention of financiers invested by an industrialist utopia, not that of engineers.

Within a few years, the word blossomed. By the 1870s, it had become a staple vocabulary to describe the nexus State/capital/engineering. Commonly described as a term of civil engineering, it would have been more accurate to refer to infrastructure as pertaining to financing and administrative law. I have also studied the syllabi and students' notes of the School of Bridges and Roads – France's principal school for engineers and civil servants in charge of designing and delivering railways – and could not find any mention of "infrastructure" until the late 19th century. Again, this absence tends to confirm the term was not one initially cherished by engineers, but one carried on by administrative law, economics, and finance.

Infrastructure entered the *Littré* dictionary in an 1886 *supplément* to the reference glossary whose first volume had been published in 1863. The publication front cover mentions that the 1886 supplementary volume to the dictionary "Holds a great number of terms of the arts, science, agriculture etc. and all kind of neologisms illustrated with examples." *Infrastructure* is defined as a "term of civil engineering. Name given to the land, the levelling work and highway structure of a railroad."

Within a few years, the term *infrastructure* had also started to appear in publications related to architecture and archaeology – then considered a single discipline.[6] It was used in a literal and non-metaphorical way to describe the foundation or buried structure, man-made or natural, of an edifice, a building, or any structure like a cave, or a monument. Novelist Jules Verne, one of the "Father of Science Fiction" also used the term in the same way in *Le Chateau des Carpathes* (1892) and *L'Île à helices* (1895).

The journey of "infrastructure" could have stopped there: a useful yet highly specialised term whose relevance was circumscribed to French engineers, archi-

5 Correspondence cited in Alfred J. Rieber, 'The Formation of La Grande Société Des Chemins de Fer Russes', *Jahrbücher Für Geschichte Osteuropas* 21, no. 3 (1973), 380.

6 Éric Alonzo, *L'Architecture de la voie* (Marseille & Champs-sur-Marne: Éditions Parenthèses & École de la ville et des territoires, 2018), 103–8.

tects, civil servants, and investors. A far-cry from the ubiquitous metaphor we know today. But that was just the beginning of a peculiar route.

The development and metamorphosis of "infrastructure" continued by way of social sciences and Marxism. From the late 1890s and throughout most of the 20th century, the denomination *infrastructure* vs. *superstructure* became a convention of French Marxist semantics to discuss Marx's approach of historical materialism. When English-speaking scholars would prefer the much more accurate *base* vs. *superstructure*, Henri Lefebvre, Louis Althusser, Michel Foucault and all francophone students of Marx embraced the semantical canon of *infrastructure* and *superstructure*. This mistranslation, and the political imaginary it conveyed have modified the meaning of "infrastructure" and amplified its impact way beyond French socialist coteries.

In 1859, Karl Marx published *Zur Kritik der Politischen Ökonomie*. Today, most commentators agree that, with the notable exception of the preface dedicated to historical materialism, this opus is a minor work mostly because all the research presented then was reworked, rewritten, enriched, and eventually published from 1867 until 1894 in Marx's magnum opus *Das Kapital*.

Yet, in the preface of his 1859 book, Marx's understanding of historical materialism is presented in a clear, short, and compelling argument. In a few words, historical materialism is the idea that an economic and technological *base* or *foundation* (Basis, in German), shapes the politics and ideology of a *superstructure* (Überbau). It clearly traces a relationship between technological or material elements on one hand, and social consciousness on the other. In Karl Marx's words:

The general conclusion at which I arrived and which, once reached, became the guiding principle of my studies can be summarized as follows. In the social production which men carry on they enter into definite relations that are indispensable and independent of their will; these relations of production correspond to a definite stage of development of their material powers of production. The sum total of these relations of production constitutes the economic structure of society – the real foundation, on which rise legal and political superstructures and to which correspond definite forms of social consciousness.[7]

When the second edition of *Zur Kritik der Politischen Ökonomie* came out in German in 1897, the work of Marx was in high demand across Europe. Two translations in French based on the second edition would be published in 1899 and 1909. Yet, none of them used the term of *infrastructure*. So how did the work become a topos of francophone Marxist literature? It is also worth noting that at the time, its literary value was almost immediately disputed – was Marx's *infrastructure* to be considered literally or metaphorically? I have tracked "infrastructure" across time and languages, and can confidently propose one hypothesis: the concept of "infrastructure" – this phrase, this figure of speech – is down to the creativity of one individual.

7 Karl Marx, *A Contribution to the Critique of Political Economy*, trans. Nahum Isaac Stone (Chicago: Charles H. Kerr Company, 1904), 11.

In 1897, George Sorel (1847–1922) was a leading personality of French Socialism and a peculiar figure in the French intellectual landscape. A self-taught theoretician and polymath, Georges Sorel had resigned from the civil service in 1892 and had emerged out of nowhere as an atypical figure of socialism. Sorel is especially interesting to us, because of his training and professional career. A graduate of the School of Bridges and Roads and École Polytechnique, Sorel spent most of his civil service career delivering and managing railways. By studying a series of writings Sorel published between 1895 and 1897, that I will not review in detail here, we can witness how he "metaphorised" *infrastructure* and effortlessly brought it into socialist parlance, where it became a canon of Marxism and social sciences. This transformation is especially striking in an 1895 critical review titled "The Theories of Mr. Durkheim" where Sorel used the word *infrastructure* to describe the most profound sediments of social phenomena. And then in a footnote where he justifies his use of *infrastructure* in such an atypical context, he writes:

Architecture provides a good illustration: the shapes of buildings, their ornaments, what is the most visible, constitute the elements on which your average thinker bases their thinking; – quite the opposite, history deals with modes of construction, technical processes, assemblage of materials. In archaeological treatises produced by professors, the former point of view is the one that prevails. Artists are more interested in the latter.[8]

In the following years, the architectural metaphor apparently coined by Sorel blossomed in the socialist circles he engaged with. At the turn of the 19th century, thanks to the literary imagination of a railway engineer, avid reader of architecture and archaeology treatises,[9] turned leading self-taught thinker of socialism, *infrastructure* quietly hijacked the debate on historical materialism and escaped its limited technical domains. The metaphor that initially pertained to Marxism slipped away almost instantly and caught up with social sciences as a successful architectural spatial metaphor.

In the early 20th century, from a figure of speech that could have remained restricted to socialist circles, "infrastructure" expanded and percolated to other disciplines. The conceptual parable was so strong, so appealing, so accurate, that it ended up building a life of its own.

It is once again important to remind ourselves of the political, intellectual, and social context of the early 20th century in Europe. Next to political movements such as socialism which called for "social consciousness", a number of "new" social sciences were emerging. Psychology, for instance, aimed at understanding the links between consciousness and subconsciousness; sociology, looked at broad trends to understand human beings as groups and what determined groups or individuals' behaviours. The image of an "infrastructure" – may it be technological, political, moral, or a dormant con-

8 Georges Sorel, 'Les Théories de M. Durkheim (Suite et Fin)', *Le Devenir Social* 1, no. 2 (May 1895), 510.

9 See Pierre Andreu, *Notre maître, M. Sorel* (Paris: Grasset, 1953), 43 where Sorel's biographer retrieved the intellectual's library borrowing statements.

sciousness – determining a "superstructure", the visible aspect of a society, would have been highly striking, fashionable, modern: it tapped into the omnipresent technical imaginary of railway expansion, while illustrating an important intellectual trend at the turn of the century. "Infrastructure" was the *zeitgeist*.

From the 1900s onwards, the use of *infrastructure* for its metaphorical value manifestly increased in French language. The relationship to Marx or socialism quickly became tenuous and it even developed outside of social sciences. Take for instance this article on functional calculus by Maximilien Winter (1871-1935), a philosopher of mathematics, published in 1913. He concludes by writing about "the infrastructure of the Universe".[10] Or this 1912 unsigned article in a periodical dedicated to music: in a concert review, the critic talks of "literary infrastructure" and later mentions the "rhythmic infrastructure" of the piece.[11] Two examples, amongst many others, of the momentum gained by the idea of infrastructure. The use of *infrastructure* became also quite distinctive in economics and would have been intrinsically linked to colonisation. As a French senator wrote in a 1919 article titled "The Colonial post-war programme"

The task that I would call the economic "equipment" of a colony is vastly more stretched that one imagines. The railway networks, the ports, the commercial navy constitute the "infrastructure", so to speak: then remains the "suprastructure" that has its importance. So that a colony can "live" with its homeland […].[12]

By the 1930s, in French, *infrastructure* had taken off to reach a whole new semantic level. From the niche technical term limited to railway engineering, architecture, and archaeology, it had blossomed. It was now more complex, used in different contexts, disciplines and by varied audiences. And it had quickly been adopted by a new transport technology: aviation. *Infrastructure* would have then described all ground equipment (airfields, airports, etc.). The same way it semantically supported the spatial project associated with railway expansion in France and its colonies, "infrastructure" now bore a similar role with the expansion of air travels. When looking at maps, for instance the "Air infrastructure of Indochina" printed in 1939, one is struck by the metonymic power of this representation: the infrastructure here, is the sum of abstract lines between Saigon and Hanoi, an illustration of the colonial project, an illustration of its modernity.

It is through aviation and defence that "infrastructure" eventually entered the English language. After the Second World War, the North Atlantic Treaty Organization (NATO) organised the defence of Europe (against the Soviet Union). A network of airfields was programmed to be built across Western Europe with most of them in France. In 1952, *The New York Times* wrote that "the word 'infrastructure', a favourite bureaucratic morsel in the language of European defence" is "baffling" to Secretary of State Dean Acheson

10 Maximilien Winter, 'Les Principes Du Calcul Fonctionnel', *Revue de Métaphysique et de Morale* (1913) 462-510.

11 Le Mois', *Revue Musicale S.I.M.* (15 January 1912).

12 Lucien Hubert, 'Le Programme Colonial d'après-Guerre', *La Revue Hebdomadaire* (30 August 1919).

(1893-1971). He was quoted saying: "One thing I can't explain to you is how these facilities came to be called by the name 'infrastructure'. But despite this heavy handicap, good progress was made on this issue, too."[13]

Once it entered the English lexicon in the 1950s, the parable of infrastructure thrived across different languages – English, German, Spanish, amongst others. The rise of development economics after the war and the establishment of their flagship institutions – the International Monetary Fund, the World Bank, the United Nations, all created in 1945 – embraced the concept of infrastructure to push the idea that a country could reach "development" by investing in fixed assets, physical networks, and equipment. The correlation between the facilities of a country – the quality of its roads, the coverage of its phone network, the resilience of its electricity grid – and its prosperity, wealth, but also its standards of moral and ethics then became more transparent. The pinnacle of the stretched use of the term "infrastructure" was arguably reached with Ronald Reagan's speech on the "infrastructure of democracy" delivered at the UK House of Commons in 1982 and which led to the creation of the National Endowment for Democracy in 1983. The apostle of free-market economics state-visiting Margaret Thatcher explained:

The objective I propose is quite simple to state: to foster the infrastructure of democracy – the system of a free press, unions, political parties, universities – which allows a people to choose their own way, to develop their own culture, to reconcile their own differences through peaceful means. This is not cultural imperialism: it is providing the means for genuine self-determination and protection for diversity.[14]

Rankings, return on investment, CAPEX, evaluation, data, metricization of space and people – the infrastructural paradigm has brought with it a cortege of jargon, tools and policy mechanisms: an infrastructural mindset that defines our political relationship to space today. I wrote this essay as a call to critically question the transparency, obviousness, the ubiquity of "infrastructure" in everyday language and social theories. If infrastructure is our "operating system" as Keller Easterling once said, we need to unpack the metaphor that defines the space we live in. Within "infraastructure" there is an association to a certain idea of progress, to technological utopia, as well as to capitalism, resources extraction and colonisation. Infrastructure as an expression of modernity crystallises an imaginary, a relation to space that we seem incapable of challenging. I hope that by uncovering the etymological journey of this term, this research can contribute prying open the semantic black box to our infrastructural age.

13 'Use of "Infrastructure" Is Baffling to Acheson', *New York Times* (1 March 1952).

14 Ronald Reagan, 'Text of President Ronald Reagan's Westminster Address – National Endowment for Democracy' (June 1982). https://www.ned.org/promoting-democracy-and-peace/.

INDEX

[de/neo/post] Colonialism

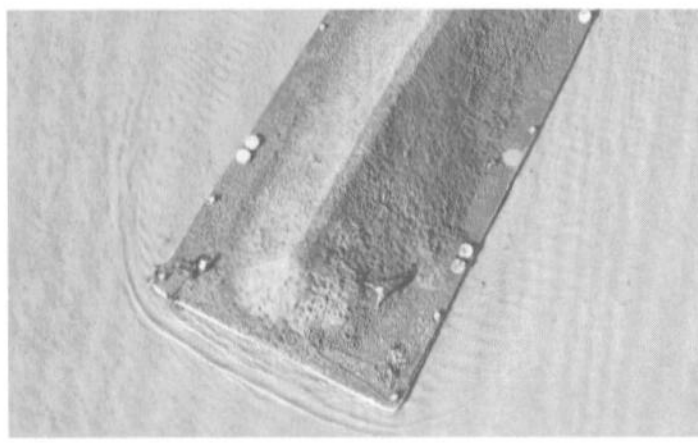

Africapitalism

Anxiety

Architectural fetishism

Benin

Blurred boundaries

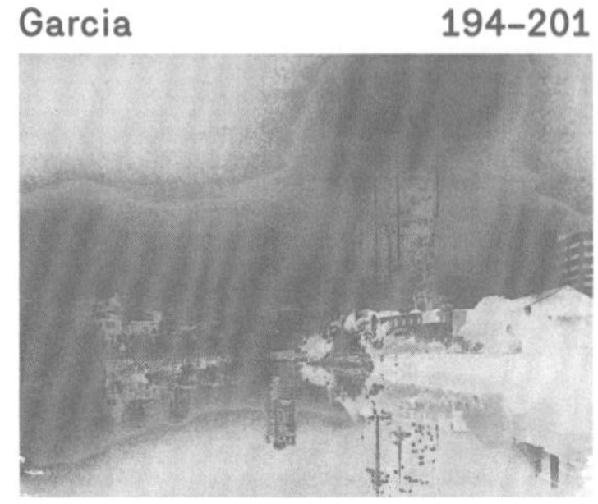

China

Collapse

Commodified nature

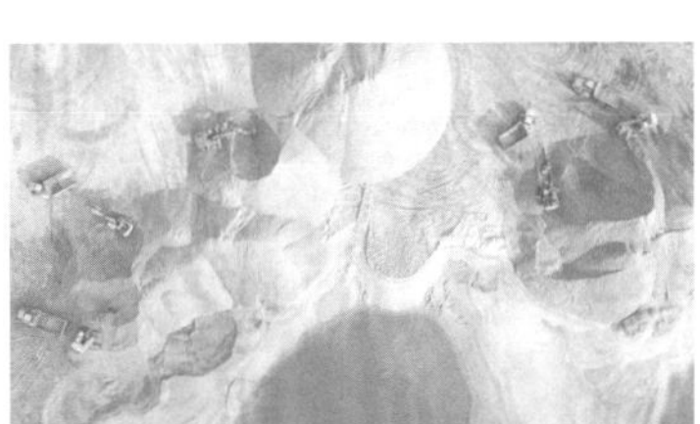

Concrete

Connected objects

Malapert 038–067
Malterre-Barthes 130–136

Vitale 164–192
Garcia 194–201

Consumerist desire

Malapert 038–067

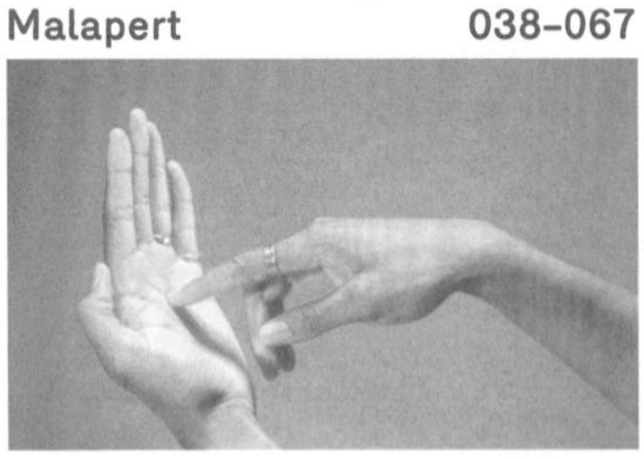

Vitale 164–192
Garcia 194–201

Death

Benjaminsen+Kimaiyo 138–163

Vitale 164–192

Straatsma 202–227

Deviance

Garcia 194–201

Gafsou 228–259

Erosion

Chi Yin 012–036

Streicher 102–128

Extraction

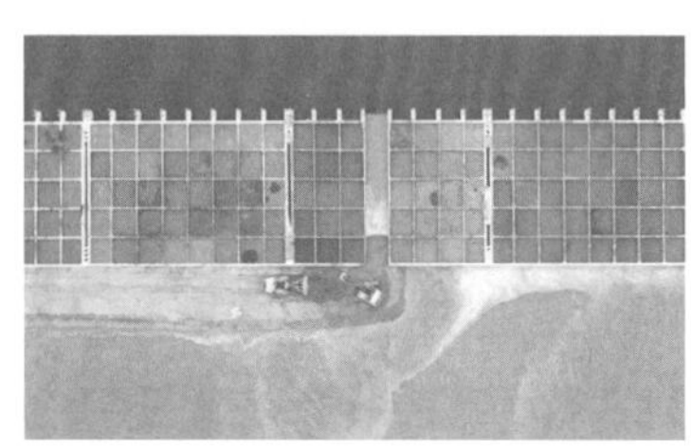

Chi Yin 012–036

Streicher 102–128
Malterre-Barthes 130–136

Fear

Offshore 074–101

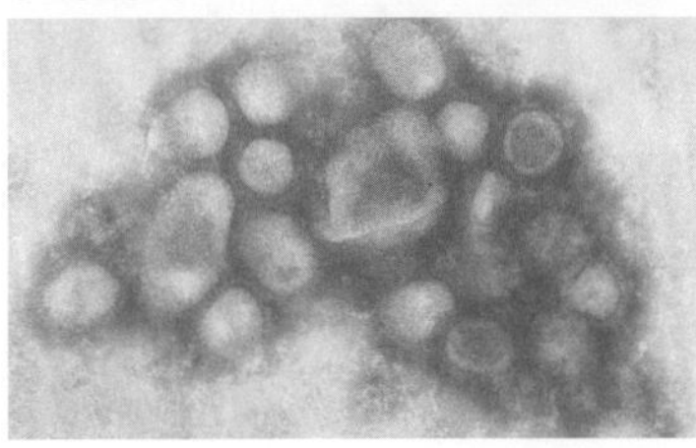

Straatsma 202–227

Financial fluxes

Chi Yin 012–036
Malterre-Barthes 130–136
Tribillon 260–268

Forests

Benjaminsen+Kimaiyo 138–163

Gafsou 228–259

Fossil fuel

Malapert 038–067
Malterre-Barthes 130–136

France

Choplin 068–072

Gafsou 228–259
Tribillon 260–268

Germany

Choplin 068–072

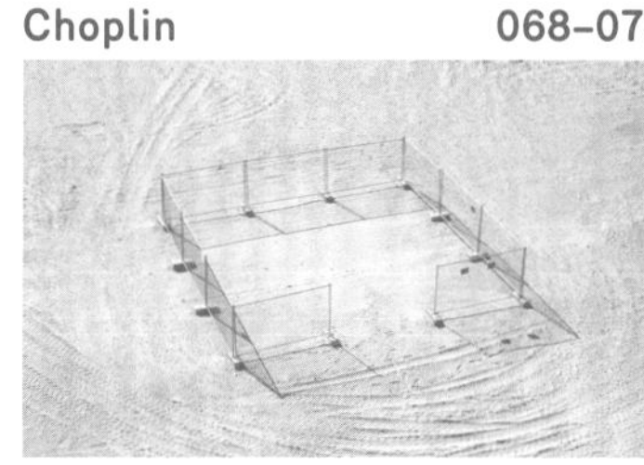

Malapert 038–067

Greenhouse gas

Choplin 068–072
Malterre-Barthes 130–136

Hegemony

Information age

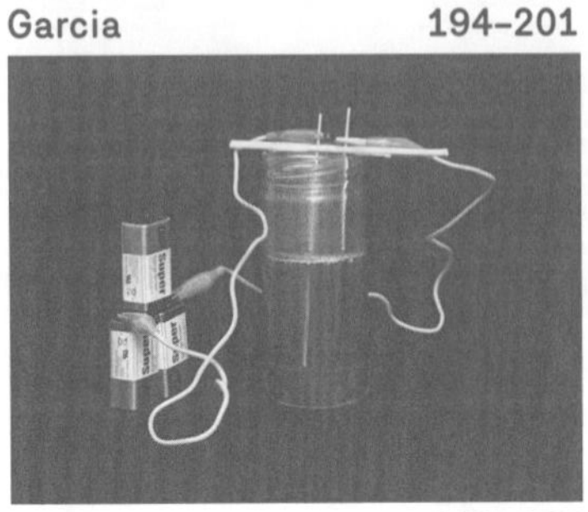

Japan

Karl Marx

Kenya

Lockdown

Lust

Malaysia

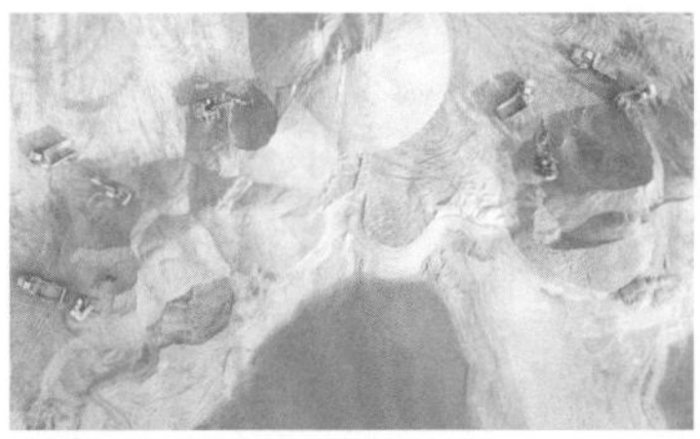

Peripheries

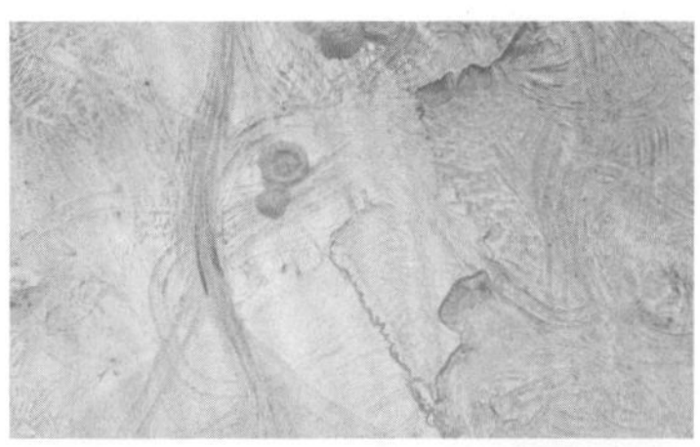

Persecution of indigenous communities

Petrol culture

Real estate

Reclamation

Chi Yin 012–036
Choplin 068–072

Malapert 038–067

Streicher 102–128
Malterre-Barthes 130–136

Réduit national

Offshore 074–101

Straatsma 202–227

Regulations

Offshore 074–101
Malterre-Barthes 130–136

Benjaminsen+Kimaiyo 138–163
Garcia 194–201

Retrofitting

Offshore 074–101
Choplin 068–072

Streicher 102–128
Malterre-Barthes 130–136

Sabotage

Vitale 164–192
Garcia 194–201

Sand

Chi Yin 012–036
Choplin 068–072

Malapert 038–067

Self-help

Offshore 074–101
Garcia 194–201

Straatsma 202–227

Sexual fetishism

Choplin 068–072
Garcia 194–201

Singapore

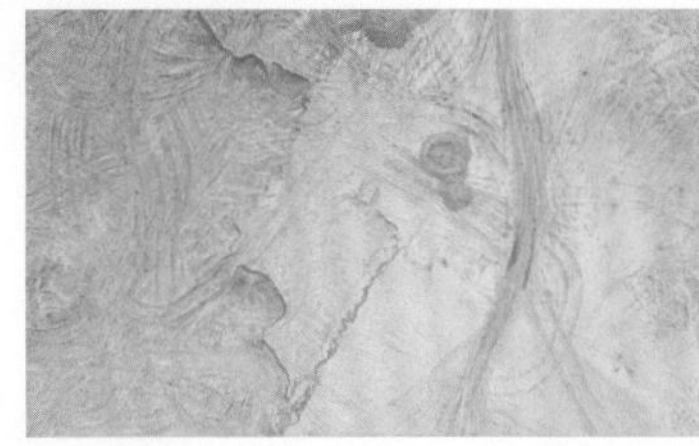

Chi Yin 012–036

South Africa

Vitale 164–192

Subsidence

Chi Yin 012–036

Streicher 102–128

Sweden

Streicher 102–128

Straatsma 202–227
Tribillon 260–268

Switzerland

Offshore 074–101
Choplin 068–072

Gafsou 228–259

Techno-solutionism

Malapert 038–067

Benjaminsen+Kimaiyo 138–163

Vitale 164–192
Garcia 194–201

The Netherlands

Straatsma 202–227

Tired bodies

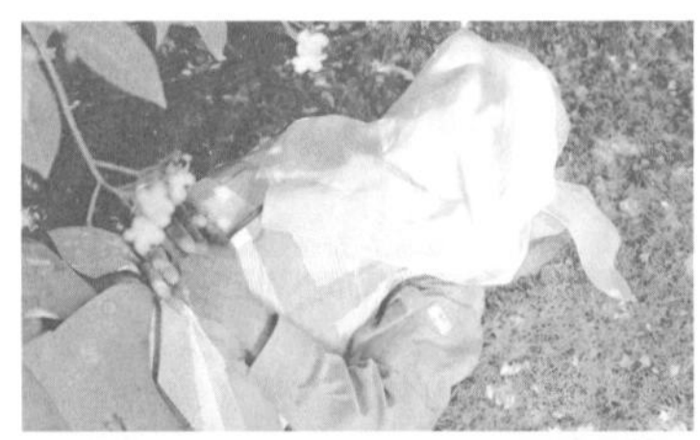

Malapert 038–067

Streicher 102–128
Malterre-Barthes 130–136

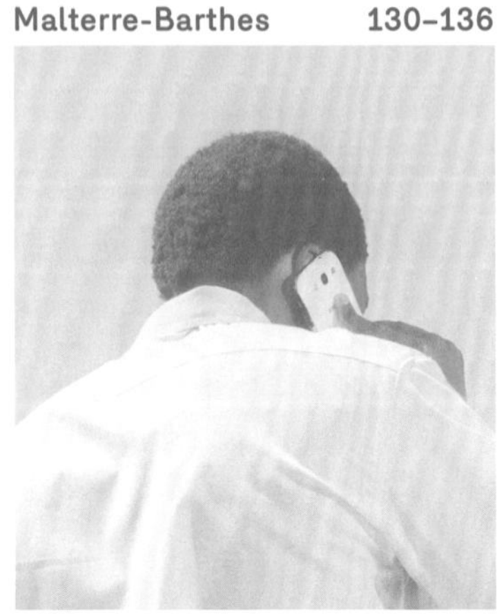

Vitale 164–192
Garcia 194–201

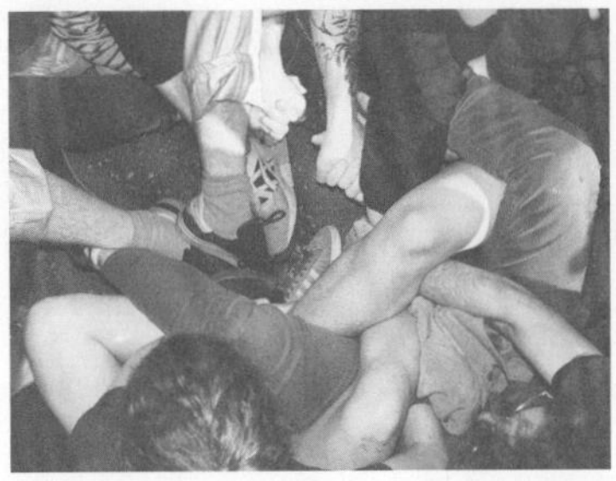

Trafficking

Trees as infrastructure

United Arab Emirates

United States of America

Vietnam

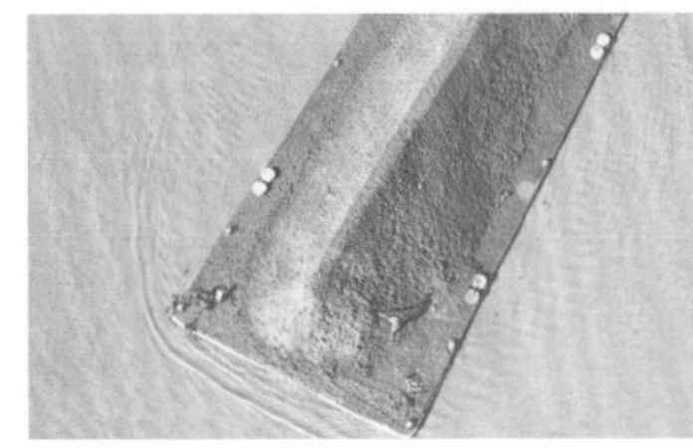

Weaponised landscape

Whorephobia

CONTRIBUTORS

ELINE BENJAMINSEN [NOR] [P.136]
is a visual artist and photographer whose work deals with the challenge of perceiving market processes and global networks through photographic investigation that combines prints, video and text in mixed-media installations. Her work has been exhibited in Amsterdam, Paris, Mannheim, The Hague, among others.

ARMELLE CHOPLIN [CHE] [P.66]
is a professor of geography and urban planning at the University of Geneva. Her research explores how cities are produced in the Global South, especially in Africa. In 2020, she published *Matière grise de l'urbain. La vie du ciment en Afrique* with Métis Presses and *Concrete City: Material Flows and Urbanization in West Africa* in 2023 (Wiley).

MATTHIEU GAFSOU [CHE] [P.228]
lives and works in Lausanne, Switzerland. A teacher at ECAL, Gafsou's work has been exhibited worldwide. In 2022, the series "Vivants" won the Ruinart Prize at Paris Photo, where the project was exhibited. In 2023 Atelier EXB published the book related to this project.

GABRIELLA GARCIA [USA] [P.192]
is a writer, performer, and poetic technologist. Her work explores the protection of radical self-expression, networked subcultures, and cybernetic intimacy. She is the co-founder and director of Decoding Stigma. Her expanded practice includes techno-feminist research/writing, collective archiving, multimedia performance art, and experiments with creative technology.

ELIAS KIMAIYO [KEN] [P.136]
is a Sengwer indigenous community leader from Embobut forest. He is also an environment, human and land rights defender as well as a community journalist. Together with other community leaders, he lobbies for ancestral land tenure rights and recognition as a distinct tribe in Kenya. Kimaiyo works closely with community allies like civil societies, journalists, researchers and paralegals.

ETIENNE MALAPERT [CHE] [P.38]
is a French photographer born in 1991 in Paris, who lives and works in Lausanne, Switzerland. He won a Swiss Design Award in 2016 for the "The City of Possibilities", published as a monograph in 2021 by art&fiction. His work has been exhibited in Arles, Lille, London, Paris, Bienne, among others.

CHARLOTTE MALTERRE-BARTHES [CHE] [P.128]
is an architect, urban designer, and assistant professor of architectural and urban design at EPFL, where she leads the laboratory RIOT. She launched in 2021 the initiative "A Global Moratorium on New Construction" urging for a profound reform of planning disciplines to face the climate and social emergency.

OFFSHORE [CHE/AUT] [P.72]
is a Zurich- and Vienna-based design studio, founded by Isabel Seiffert and Christoph Miler. Their projects focus on editorial design, typography, image-making, as well as research-driven visual narratives. Next to commissions and self-initiated research, the duo engages in design education at various European art schools. Their work has been published, exhibited and awarded internationally.

LISE STRAATSMA [NLD] [P.202]
is editorial manager of journalistic platform *De Correspondent,* based in Amsterdam. She has a background as a maker, image editor, and curator. She holds a degree in documentary photography from the Royal Academy of Art in The Hague.

KATRIN STREICHER [GER] [P.100]
is a photographer based in Berlin, Germany working on assignments for national and international media and, in parallel, on long-term personal projects. Her work has been published in *ZEIT, The New York Times, M Le Magazine du Monde*. It has been exhibited in Berlin, Hamburg, and Arles among others.

JUSTINIEN TRIBILLON [FRA] [P.8 / P.258]
is a writer, editor, and curator. He received his PhD in urban studies from The Bartlett, University College London, where he dedicated his research to the ring road of Paris. Currently a fellow at the French Academy in Rome (2023–2024), he will publish his first book as writer *The Zone: An alternative history of Paris* with Verso in the Summer of 2024.

SALVATORE VITALE [ITA/CHE] [P.162]
is an Italian Swiss-based visual artist, editor, and educator. A professor in the Transmedia storytelling programme at the Lucerne University of Applied Sciences and Arts, Vitale is the artistic director of FUTURES Photography and EXPOSED. Torino Foto Festival, as well as co-founder and editor-in-chief of *YET magazine*. His work has been exhibited in Amsterdam, London, Shanghai, Winterthur, among others.

SIM CHI YIN [SGP] [P.12]
is an artist whose research-based practice involves photography, moving images, archival interventions, book-making and performance with a focus on history, memory, conflict and extraction. From Singapore, she is currently based in New York where she was a fellow in the Whitney Independent Study programme (2022–2023) and a PhD candidate at King's College London.

EDITED BY
Isabel Seiffert, Christoph Miler,
Justinien Tribillon

COPY-EDITING
Justinien Tribillon

PROOFING
Frederik von Richthofen

DESIGN
Offshore:
Isabel Seiffert and
Christoph Miler
offshorestudio.ch

PRINTING AND BINDING
Longo AG
Johann Kravogl Straße 7
39100 Bozen

PAPER
Profitop Opak 1.1, 80 gsm
Gray cardboard 0.32 mm

TYPEFACES
Rev-G by Selina Bernet
Merkury by Radim Peško
Publico Mono by Commercial Type

PUBLISHER
Spector Books
Harkortstrasse 10
04107 Leipzig
www.spectorbooks.com

DISTRIBUTION
Germany, Austria: GVA,
Gemeinsame
Verlagsauslieferung
Göttingen GmbH&Co. KG,
www.gva-verlage.de
Switzerland: AVA
Verlagsauslieferung AG,
www.ava.ch
France, Belgium: Interart Paris,
www.interart.fr
UK: Central Books Ltd,
www.centralbooks.com
USA, Canada, Central and South America,
Africa: ARTBOOK/ D.A.P.,
www.artbook.com
South Korea: The Book Society,
www.thebooksociety.org
Japan: twelvebooks,
www.twelve-books.com
Australia, New Zealand:
Perimeter Distribution,
www.perimeterdistribution.com

IMAGE CREDITS
Cover Offshore, 2021
P.76 ETH Image Library; photo: Hans Röthlisberger
P.78 ETH Image Library, 1895
P.79 Wikimedia Commons
P.80 Federal library, military postcard collection of the library Guisanplatz, Bern, Switzerland. Illustration by Eric de Coulon.
P.81 Wikimedia Commons, image by user "Paebi"
P.82 ETH Image Library
P.83 "Die Gotthardfestung San Carlo, der Prototyp aller Artilleriewerke mit 10,5 cm Turm-Kanonen Mod 1939 L52", © Fischerdörfli-Verlag, Hansjakob Burkhardt
P.84 Wikimedia Commons, image by user "Paebi"
P.85 Federal library, military postcard collection of the library Guisanplatz, Bern, Switzerland. Illustration by Eric de Coulon.
P.86 Swiss Federal Archives, E5792#1988/204#1302*, 1939–1945.
P.87 Swiss Data Safe AG, www.swissdatasafe.ch
P.88,89 Rechenzentrum Stollen Luzern, www.rz-stollen.ch
P.91 Federal Media Library, Swiss Defense Department
P.93 swissmountainfortress.com

First Edition, 2024
Printed in Italy

ISBN 978-3-95905-755-4

Special thanks to: Caroline Courrioux, Sam Stourdzé, Amélie Samson, Gabriele Onere, Selina Bernet, iloveimg.com, Sigrid Schmeisser, Salvatore Vitale, Billie the Dog

Next two images: 3D-rendering and floor plan for the exhibition that never happened: *Visible upon breakdown* at the photo festival Les Rencontres d'Arles in 2021 and 2020.

With the support of
prohelvetia
ERNST GÖHNER STIFTUNG

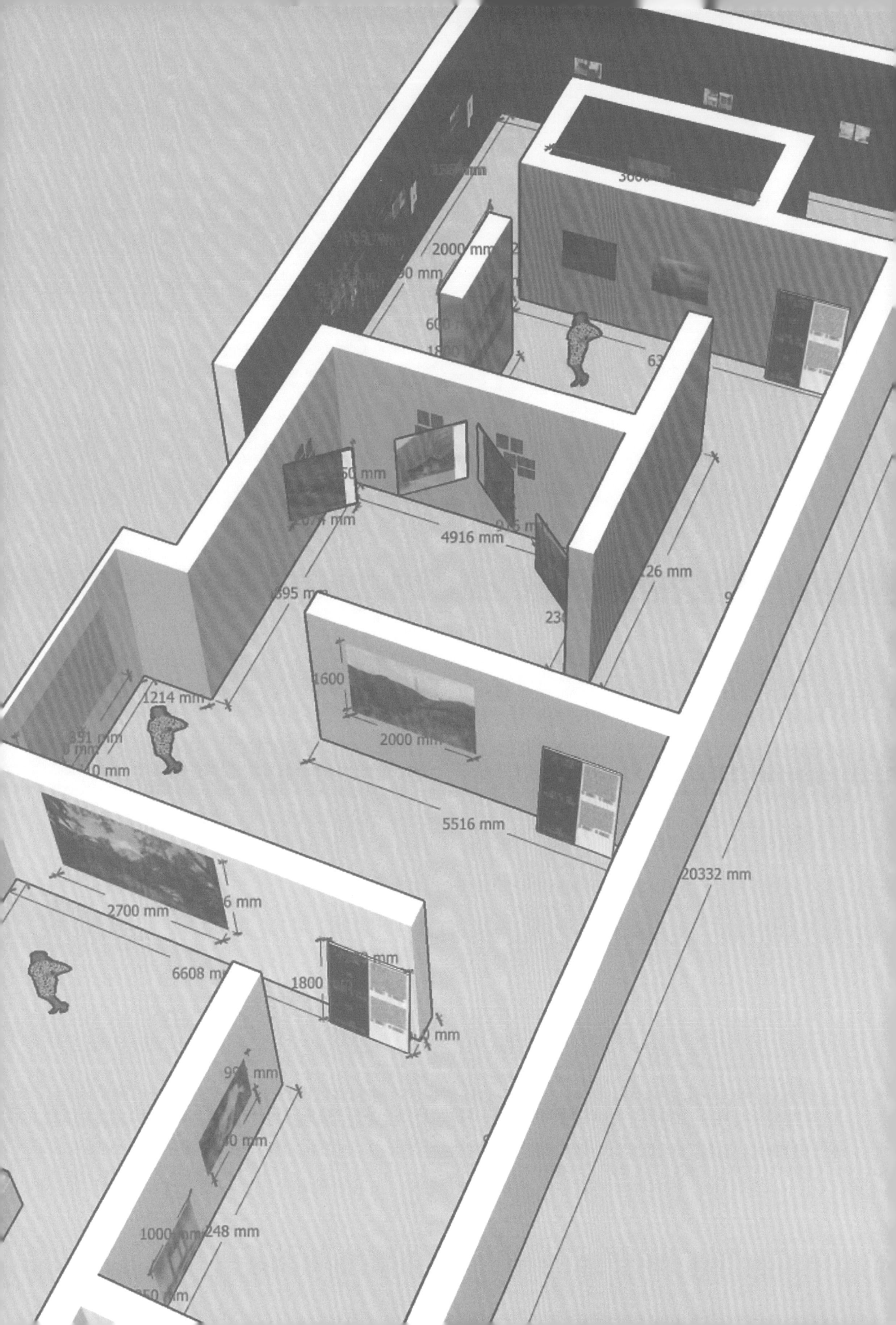
2000 mm
4916 mm
1600
1214 mm
2000 mm
5516 mm
2700 mm
1800
20332 mm

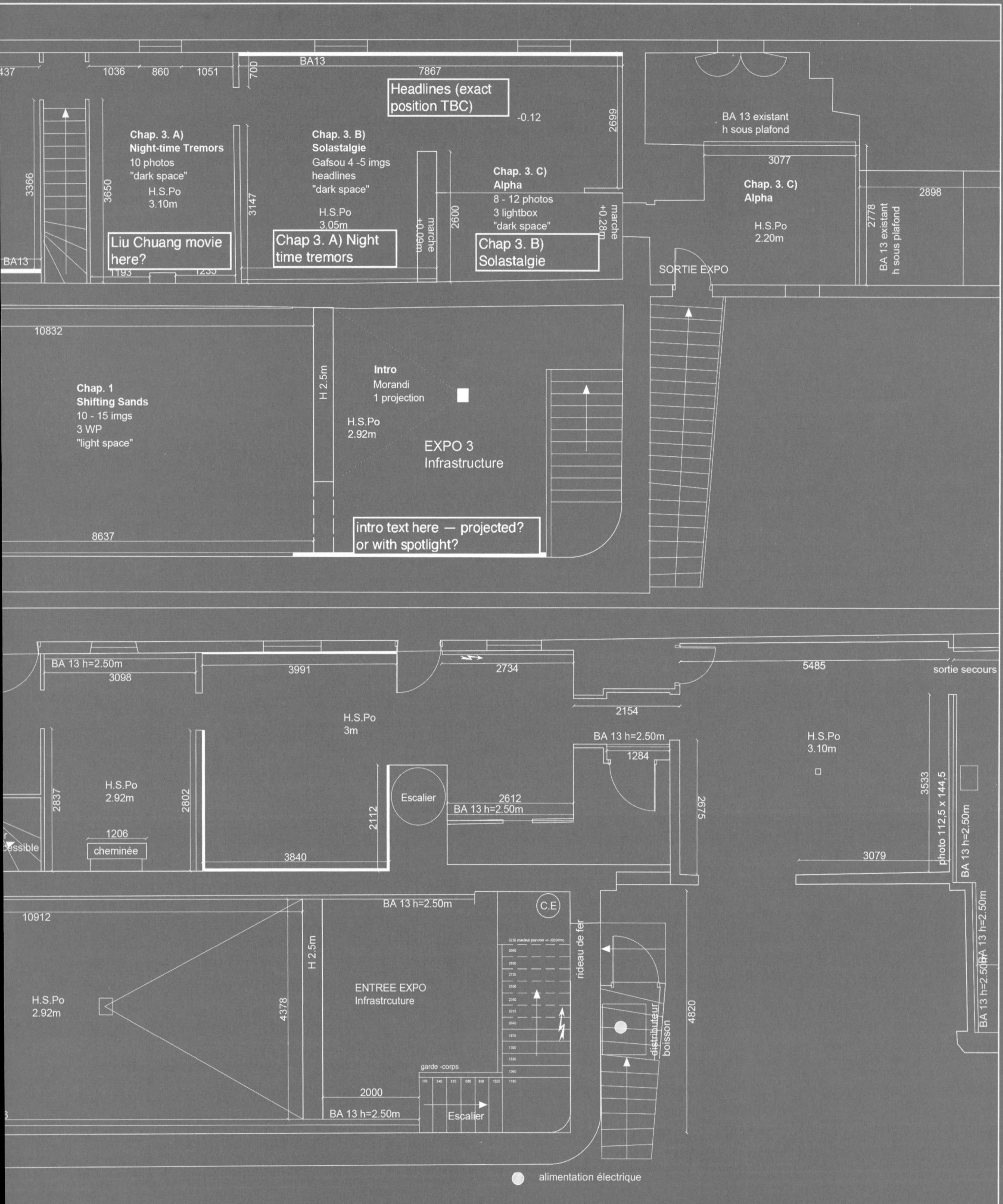

MAISON DES PEINTRES - Appartement et Garage

01	S=390m²
/100@A3	
/19	

EXPOSITION :
INFRASTRUCTURE / RANDA MAROUFI / UNE ATTENTION PARTICULIÈRE
COMMISSAIRES :
XXXX
PRODUCTION:
XXX

16 A rigid-hull, inflatable boat helps search for survivors of the capsized commercial passenger ferry *MV Princess of the Stars*, June 25. The ferry capsized during Typhoon Fengshen in the Philippines. Source: US Navy.

17 On 25 August 2005, following hurricane Katrina, there were over 50 failures of the levees and flood walls protecting New Orleans and its suburbs. The failures caused flooding in 80% of New Orleans and all of St. Bernard Parish. In New Orleans alone, 134,000 housing units suffered damage.

18 *One Apus* arrives in Kobe, Japan on 8 December 2020, after losing an estimated 1,816 containers in the Pacific Ocean. Source: WK Webster Group, Press Video.

19 The 1975 Banqiao Dam failure was the collapse of the Banqiao Dam and 61 other dams in Henan, China, under the influence of typhoon Nina in August 1975. The dam collapse created the third deadliest flood in history which affected a population of 10.15 million, inundated around 30 cities and killed more than 26,000 people.

20 A HV transmission tower that collapsed after severe storms rolled through the northeast side of San Antonio, where some winds reached 177 kmh with four confirmed tornadoes, February 2017. Source: insulators.info, Mike Jordan

21 In the 1960s, the Corona spy satellite system was launched with a total of 144 US satellites under a top-secret Cold War project. These satellites used ground markers to calibrate their cameras and many of them remain in the Arizona desert. Source: Google Earth.

22 Smoke rises from the Fukushima Daiichi nuclear reactor (Unit 1) after an explosion, 15 March 2011. Source: Nippon Television Network Corporation.

23 Cloud seeding at Corryong, Australia, with a Cessna 320 airplane in 1966. Seeding artificial clouds achieved rainfall increases as high as 30% in autumn. Source: Forests Commission Victoria.

24 An antenna coloured to blend in with its host building, in Sopot, Poland. Source: Wikimedia Commons, Pplecke.

25 In Kuwait City's Sulaibiya area gigantic holes are dug out and filled with old tires. There are now over seven million in the ground and the patches are even visible from space. In 2021, Kuwait started to burn parts of the tires in factories close to the border to Saudi Arabia to produce oil for industrial furnaces. Source: Google Earth.

26 Parts of the Rhone Glacier are covered under blankets to slow down the melting process and keep open the manmade tunnel system underneath for tourists. Switzerland, 2021. Source: Offshore.

27 The border fence between El Paso and Juarez has an elaborate gate structure to allow floodwaters to pass under. The grates prevent people from crossing but can be raised for floodwaters carrying chunks of debris. Source: Wikipedia, Dicklyon.

28 Unfinished houses in La Coruña, during the global financial crises in 2008. The Spanish property bubble bursted in various stages from 1985 up to 2008. Source: Wikimedia Commons, Xenokrates.

29 Cell tower disguised as a palm tree, a common structure that is also nicknamed "monopalm", 2007. Source: Reddit.

30 US Navy RH-53Ds sweeping the Suez Canal during the mine clearing operation in 1974. Following the Yom Kippur War between Egypt and Israel, an agreement was reached in October 1973 to clear and reopen the canal since it provides a crucial passage for global shipping and trade. Source: US navy.

31 Transport of a tripods foundation for offshore wind farms in Wilhelmshaven, Germany, 2008. Source: Image Archive Alpha Venture.

16

17

18

19

20

21

22

23